MOTHERHOOD
and Other Natural Disasters

Jan Blackburn

Inspiring Voices®
A Service of **Guideposts**

Inspiring Voices books may be ordered through booksellers or by contacting:

Inspiring Voices
1663 Liberty Drive
Bloomington, IN 47403
www.inspiringvoices.com
1-(866) 697-5313

Illustrations provided by Sue Davidson and printed with permission.

ISBN: 978-1-4624-0476-6 (sc)
ISBN: 978-1-4624-0475-9 (e)

Library of Congress Control Number: 2012923759

Printed in the United States of America

Inspiring Voices rev. date: 01/23/2013

Introduction

When I was a young girl I used to enjoy writing short stories; at the time I called them novels. Behind me lived a girl my age that actually enjoyed reading my musings. No matter how atrocious the stories, she always pronounced them wonderful

One year as adults we met at the funeral of a mutual friend. After exchanging the usual pleasantries, she looked me square in the eye and said, "I'm so disappointed in your life!"

I was taken somewhat aback by her blatant honesty, but after considering her comment for a second, I replied, "Yeah, me too. Which part of my life are you disappointed in?"

"I always thought that you would grow up to be a great writer," she told me. "I looked forward to buying your books."

"So did I," was my comment and after thinking about it for a long time I realized finally what I wanted to be when I grew up. But at forty years of age I wondered if it was too late to start over. When I pulled the manuscript out again in my fifties the same questions still laid in my heart and mind. But at some point you have to stop dreaming about what you wish you could do and actually make an effort to do it.

So here's my first effort. Since it took 20+ years to write it I may not live long enough for a second book so you'd better enjoy this one!

Special thanks to my kids Nick and Jake and for their friends for giving me such rich material to write about. They once threatened to sue me for defamation of character should I ever publish this book; I hope they have forgotten that threat and will instead enjoy reliving their childhoods through my eyes. Extra special thanks to both my first husband Jeff and my current husband Mike for sharing the priceless experience of parenting and for just generally putting up with me through all the stages of life and love.

Thanks to Julie Wells who patiently listened to the finished product after I wrote each chapter, who laughed and cried with me and who added so many stories to the mix… "Bet I can top *that!*"

Special thanks to Diane Guntrip, Tammy Stevenson, and Jana Plummer for helping me look for the original cartoon that was to be the cover of the book. It turned into the search for the Holy Grail and ended as a 20+ year old "needle in a haystack" that refused to be found. Special appreciation and thanks to the library staff at the Hicks Undergraduate Library at Purdue University in West Lafayette for going above and beyond in trying to assist me in my search for this same cartoon.

Extra special thanks to my best friend Sue Davidson who drew the wonderful cartoon that became the cover. It's actually even better because it almost looks like me, and depicts my two sons and the two dogs that helped herd my children. Thanks also to Heather Steele who helped with digitally colorizing the image for the cover.

I also pray God's richest blessings to the entire staff of Inspiring Voices for their invaluable advice, patience, endurance and support in guiding me through this first publishing experience.

Lastly and most importantly, I couldn't have written this book without the stories of parents who shared their experiences as well. Thanks to all for allowing me share your stories as well as my own.

My children grew a lot during the writing of this book-hopefully so did I.

Table of Contents

Chapter 1
Looking for Harriet Nelson

I find myself watching reruns of the 1960s television series *Ozzie and Harriet* with a sense of longing. What interests me the most are the sequences where Harriet and her neighbor sit at the kitchen table enjoying fresh cookies from the oven while drinking coffee. They obviously enjoy a close friendship and have time to share the details of their lives. Their families are the center of their existence, and they truly seem to enjoy life just that way.

Harriet Nelson, June Cleaver, and, later, Marion Cunningham were our television heroines, embodying the characteristics of the wife and mother I believed I would someday be. Somewhere along the line I was misinformed. Instead of joining the time-honored profession of motherhood full-time, I find I am squeezing it in between housework, personal interests, and a part-time career. Sharing intimate details of my life is no longer done with friends on a face-to-face basis. Rather, it is something done over the telephone, on e-mail, or on Facebook, usually while I am doing the dishes or laundry. In reading a book on parenting, I found an anonymous quote that aptly describes the parenting experience: "Parenting is something that happens while you are busy doing something else."

You never once saw Harriet Nelson come tearing out of the

house, her clothes half-buttoned, her hair mussed, without make-up, and hollering, "Come on, kids, we're late!" Harriet Nelson was always on time. I, however, am a different story. Once upon a time, I too was punctual, sometimes even arriving at my destination a few minutes early. That was "BC," Before Children. Now I am either barely on time or notoriously late. If church starts at ten o'clock a.m., I can be counted on to slide down the aisle and skid into the pew with less than thirty seconds until showtime. In fact, for awhile the congregation mistook me for a deacon, because I always seemed to follow the pastor down the aisle!

Once I wore that fine makeup "sold only in department stores." Now, if I have time to put on makeup at all, I find myself digging out the last drops with a Q-Tip, making Mr. Scrooge look like a philanthropist. Once I thought that buying clothes from K-Mart was as contemptible as buying them from a rummage sale. Now I find either alternative acceptable; I'm simply glad to have something new to wear, regardless of where it came from!

I find myself alternately amused and disgusted by the television commercials in which young models complain about those tiny lines around their eyes. They recommend using their miracle anti-age cream, with an unspoken promise: "You, too, can look as good as me while you are complaining." Well, perhaps all *she* needs is Oil of Olay, but I am pretty sure the only thing that will fill in these cracks is plaster of paris, or perhaps surgery.

Thanks to my two lovely children, my once thin, lithe body has been replaced by a physique that any Sumo wrestler would be proud of. It would seem that my prenatal cravings did not stop with the cutting of the umbilical cord. Instead, the cravings have become more defined; I don't eat as much—just more often. Instead of inhaling the whole pizza, I find I can now restrain myself to five or six pieces!

Prior to children, the word *diet* was a foreign language, and overweight was a disease process that happened only to others. The concept of dieting has now become a permanent shadow, lurking around corners and staring accusingly at me just as I am about to dive into that heavenly turtle cheesecake. I can almost hear my conscience speak to me, in a voice that sounds just like a Jewish mother's: "Well, *that* will cost you a thousand sit-ups" or "Why don't you just rub it into your hips? That's where it will go anyway!" I am beginning to understand how Pinocchio must have felt with Jiminy Cricket as his conscience, always trying to keep him out of trouble. I find myself wanting to bind and gag that still small voice that reminds me that Goodyear called this morning to see if they could use my body for blimp advertisements.

Surgery is definitely an option, but by the time they lift my face, augment my breasts, and suck the fat out of my hips, thighs, and belly, the national debt will seem a small price to pay in comparison.

Remember those carefree days of youth when you could lounge in a hot bubble bath, reading a sleazy novel while sipping an ice-cold cola? Me neither, but I know I used to do it. Now, invariably, someone comes in while I am bathing, lets all the warm air out of the bathroom, stinks up the room, finishes my Coke, and leaves me with an empty glass in a cold room you can't breathe in. If I'm lucky, at least the book stays dry.

The bathroom has become a convention center, and no matter when I enter my "office," it isn't long before someone is knocking on the door asking how much longer I will be in there. I don't care what time of day I try to have a few moments of privacy (and believe me, I've tried them all), someone inevitably knocks on the door, indicating a need for relief that somehow always exceeds my own. I have even tried leaving the lights off in the hope that they won't find me, but alas, they always do.

I can't prove it, but I believe my son may be selling tickets to the bathroom. One day, one of my neighbor's sons sauntered into it, saying he had been advised by my son that it was "okay" to come in. I would not have felt so bad except that when I came out of the bathroom, I found my son leaning up against the wall, wearing a maroon leather jacket and chewing a toothpick, looking like a Hollywood pimp. I tell you, the kid's watching too much television!

"I'd like to trade my 15 minutes of fame for 15 minutes of peace in the bathroom without any kids pounding on the door."

Chapter 2

"Super-Woman Syndrome," aka Every Woman Is a Working Woman

In the 1960s and '70s, women began to come into their own. Every cause and industry, from music to cosmetics, realized that women represented heretofore untapped wealth for political and commercial change. Women were working in increasing numbers—they had their own money. They had their own minds. They had their own *power*. Every industry began to ramp up their advertising campaigns specifically targeting the fairer sex. Their message, "You Can Have It All," led to a philosophy known as "Superwoman Syndrome." In the 1980s we honestly believed in the concept, knocking ourselves out trying to catch that elusive butterfly. To the younger women following in the same belief, we will tell you now:

You can have it all!

All of the laundry, all of the cleaning, all of the childcare, and a full-time job as well. Most of the millions of American women currently employed outside the home feel disillusioned, disappointed, and discouraged about their role as women.

As a budding young feminist, I was thrilled when I heard mentors like Helen Reddy, Gloria Steinem, and Jane Fonda urging us to embrace the fact that we were women, telling us that we should raise our voices and let the world hear from us, an emerging power too smart to ever return to the repression of previous generations.

Well, I guess three out of four isn't too bad. I *am* woman, there are *a lot* of us, and we are pretty smart. However, the only thing I'm roaring about these days is how those darned toys get back out into the middle of the living room floor so soon after I pick them up. I swear I can pick up the toys, come back five minutes later, and find they have miraculously reappeared in the middle of the floor. I believe they must walk back on their own, for the children always deny they had anything to do with it, and the dog moves only when there is a hot prospect in the garbage can she wants to investigate.

I find that the oft-repeated activities comprising "domestic bliss" leave me unsure at times whether I am coming or going, a condition I like to call "Shooting Gallery Syndrome." You start to do the dishes, when—*bing*—the phone rings. After you ascertain that you really do not need new replacement windows, and, finding yourself unable to remember what you were doing before the phone rang, you start off to the laundry room—*bing*—the baby starts to cry. On your way to check the baby—*bing*—well, you know the rest of the story. Pretty soon you find yourself just like that poor little duck in the shooting gallery, perpetually doomed to travel back and forth along the same track, changing direction every time you are hit. When all is said and done, you are left devoid of brain cells, energy, or even the ability to speak in sentences containing more than four-letter words.

Anyone who says that full-time mothers are not working women should try it for six months. Most of the working women I know are thrilled to return to work after a two-week hiatus with their families. It is not that they like their jobs any better. It is simply that at least at work they enjoy respect and dignity among their peers, and their opinions have validity. They commiserate about their frustrations of being a wife and mother with one another. They can even talk about religion and politics without being ridiculed by their husbands. Where does the full-time mom go to vent her steam? Certainly *not* with her husband—*he* is usually part of the problem!

In recent years, full-time moms have been viewed as second-class citizens, as if by opting to stay home they have chosen to be lazy and unfulfilled. Well, I don't know about you, but I work harder on my days at home than I *ever* do at work! The phrase "just a housewife" should be stricken from our vocabularies.

If the full-time mom were given medals for each job she performs, she would be decorated more grandly than a four-star general. To be a mom, you must be a chef, a teacher, a housekeeper, a counselor, a lawyer, a nurse, a social worker, a referee, a chauffer, a cheerleader, a minister, and, in your spare time, a friend and lover to your spouse or significant other. The full-time mom has little time to watch television and eat bonbons, contrary to the picture we have painted of her. The working mother, due to time constraints, plays an abbreviated version of the above. She simply does not have the time to do it all. Therefore, she usually feels disjointed, as if she never gets to finish anything. On weeks when I am gone from home a lot, I often feel like I am the babysitter and she is their true parent.

I don't need to be a psychologist to sense the resentment my children feel about my job. It is really tough to walk away from a child with tear-filled eyes, who sadly says, "Please don't leave me today, Mommy!" I climb back into my car and head to work, feeling selfish and sad about leaving them. Without saying a word, I have left no doubt in their minds where they are on my priority list.

The workplace does not help the situation. The medical profession can be a terrible place to work when you have a family. As a nurse, I have found that "flexibility" must be your middle name. You may work any and all shifts, including weekends and holidays. You may be called in on your day off, or called off with little or no pay, and with little advance warning. Indeed, most of the jobs listed as having "flexible scheduling" means that it is *you,* not they, who will have to be flexible!

The most important person in your life becomes your babysitter. Her ability to be flexible must match your own. Most day care centers cannot provide that. Many private babysitters have families of their own, with their own needs to consider.

The most priceless and rare find is the babysitter who comes to your home. There the children at least have their own beds, toys, and surroundings. The thing I hated most about working twelve-hour shifts was waking my children at five or six o'clock in the morning, bundling them up, and dragging them out on a cold winter morning, usually without breakfast—talk about *guilt!*

The babysitter may indeed be invaluable, but her pay scale usually does not reflect that. While I paid 20–25 percent of my weekly income to a babysitter, she would still have to care for more children to make enough money to make ends meet. The more children a babysitter cares for, the less individualized attention any one child can hope to obtain.

Most double-income families argue that they need both incomes to survive. Indeed, inflation is a factor to be reckoned with, but we seem to be approaching the problem from the wrong direction. Since millions of dollars are being spent trying to correct deficiencies and problems caused by the lack of parental direction, perhaps the government should provide improved incentives for single-income families. If the incentives are great enough, then perhaps those moms who work purely for the income would be free to return home once more. Moms leaving the workforce would open up jobs for currently unemployed family heads. Remaining women in the workforce would be those truly in financial need and/or those who just plain want to work for their own personal reasons.

I realize there are inherent flaws even in my own brilliant philosophy. For one thing, there will always be double-income families who will do so to enjoy more of those material things associated with the "good life." Never in the history of this country have so many serious crimes been committed by mere children. Drug abuse and teenage pregnancy have reached epidemic proportions and are starting at earlier ages. In our zeal to provide our children with the very best of material goods, our very absence to acquire those things creates a bigger problem. The large blocks of unsupervised time and lack of organized activity can leave children with a void that they must struggle to fill on their own. Some will find their niche in sports or academics. Others will follow the path of least resistance, following whatever crowd gives them their greatest sense of worth and acceptance. Maintaining that acceptance sometimes comes at the expense of sacrificing their ideals and values to the accepted norm of the chosen group. To go against the crowd is to risk expulsion at a time when rejection is unthinkable. Much like adult life, isn't it?

By their own admission, this is how some cults do their recruiting—by selecting kids who are undirected and easily led. Cults such as satanic worship have increased in numbers even in rural communities. I was appalled to learn that Satanism occurs even in our tiny town. A raid on the lockers of the junior high school a few years ago resulted in the acquisition of at least six Satanic Bibles! Our local fire inspector, who has become very interested in investigating cult activities in our area, reports he was advised by an employee of a major bookstore chain that they have had great difficulty keeping up with the demand for the Satanic Bible. It seems to be one of the fastest-moving books on the market. Children are taught about cults and mystic groups openly in today's school systems yet must go off campus to learn about God and religion. Now to me, we are talking about the same things. Since Satanism is a religious choice, then it seems that if one religion is banned from the system, then so should they all be. It seems to me that the rule about "separation of church and state" has become a very one-sided issue. I wonder how long it will be before some antichurch zealot will insist that "In God We Trust" be omitted from our national coinage. It seems we have forgotten the very reason our country was founded. We have only to look at other nations of the world to see why we should fight to keep what our forefathers worked so hard to provide for us.

The other flaw in my "stay at home" theory is that most of us who have devoted many years to a craft or profession haven't the vaguest idea what we would do at home on a continuing basis. The thought of full-time cooking and cleaning (two things I don't enjoy *any* time) is terrifying. Those of us considering a return to the domestic front should have a reorientation class much like the ones people take when they reenter the workforce.

Perhaps what we really need is a return to the activities of yesteryear. Once women had "sewing circles" where they could gather and exchange ideas and recipes while doing jobs they might have found less entertaining if done while alone. The same things could easily be done among women of all ages. Unlike in days of yore, today's woman has become reliant on quick microwave dishes and instant mixes. The only time I get old-time home cooking is when I go to family reunions or church dinners. Some of those older ladies sure can cook! So maybe that is what we need: an opportunity for them to share the benefit of their experience, and an opportunity for us to learn things we might otherwise never have the chance to learn. Both generations have something to gain—the older generation to prove to themselves and others that they still have worth, and the younger generation to gain valuable skills that may otherwise become extinct.

Additionally, it gives us the opportunity to truly get to know one another again. Maybe that is what is missing from today's world. We have no time to develop relationships with anyone. I barely know my neighbors. It really isn't that I am a snob—I am just never home.

Our community has never been the same since the schools consolidated in the 1960s. Prior to that time, 90 percent of daily activities occurred within a small radius. Now the town has dwindled to a small burg. The school and most of the businesses have moved to larger towns or have disappeared completely. Now most of what we need must be obtained elsewhere. The sense of community-mindedness is generally a thing of the past. I think we have lost something terribly important.

Chapter 3

"Give Me Liberty or Give Me Children— Uh, I Mean Death!"

As a young child, I played for hours with my dolls, loving them, nurturing them, and, like my mother before me, encouraging them to "be all they could be." I am sure if my Raggedy Ann or Zip the Monkey could talk, they would tell you I was always warm, compassionate, and understanding. I honestly believed I would be a wonderful mother, and (probably also like my mother before me) I labored under the misconception that my children would always tell me everything because I was so open-minded. I knew in my heart that I would always take time for my children. Finally, in later adolescence, when I became more well-rounded in my all-knowingness, I vowed I would never say "I'm too tired" to my husband. Isn't it amazing how reality blows holes in your delusions?

To tell the truth, I find the angelic halo I had associated with motherhood has slipped just left of center. I had neglected to realize a few key points:

1. Raggedy Ann could not talk. Therefore, I never once heard her scream, "I hate you!" or "You're so mean!" She

never back-talked me once and never called me "Mommy Dearest."

2. In all the years Zip the Monkey was my constant companion, he never once tried to humiliate me by throwing himself on the floor at Walmart, swore in front of Grandma, or had himself evicted from a preschool program for bad behavior.

In the final analysis, it seems I was ill prepared for parenting. I find, however, that I am joined by several million other parents, who, like me, never received a complimentary instruction manual with their little bundles of joy.

Why is it that I have an instruction manual for every appliance in my house, and yet not even a hint of an instruction for something as important as child rearing? I guess, come to think of it, that is not entirely true. Everyone seems to have a little piece of advice on the most fool-proof method of dealing with children. I've really come to hate sentences that begin with "Well, if he were *my* child …"

I guess I had it coming, though. As a young adult I used to look at parents whose kids were throwing fits at 125 decibels and mutter, "No child of *mine* will *ever* act like that!" I was right—mine were even worse!

Temper tantrums in public places leave a parent in a "Catch-22" situation. If you don't personally flog the daylights out of the offender, someone thinks you are too permissive. However, if you opt to flatten the little monster, some conscientious soul whips out the toll-free number for the local child-abuse hotline. You just can't win at the parenting game.

I recently read an article citing fifty things you should never to do your child, lest you screw them up in perpetuity. Of the fifty, the only faux pas I had *not* committed was #37—*Never humiliate your child in public*. It is not because I am a quality parent that I avoided this parental no-no; rather, it is because when they were younger I tried not to be seen in public with them at all. I learned early on that to include them anywhere I would have contact with other adults is an open invitation for them to humiliate *me* in public!

I hated shopping with young children. Not only did I usually not get what I went shopping for in the first place, but I often ended up buying things I didn't intend to buy.

My children are not the timid, shy kind who clings to your side in a store. Their minds (and feet) run a hundred miles an hour, trying to take in all the sights. Their hands must touch everything, as if some magic braille will give them the answers they seek. With both of them going opposite directions the moment we hit the door, it is impossible to keep an eye on them and shop at the same time. In short, they are a shopkeeper's worst nightmare.

One day I made the fatal mistake of taking them with me when visiting a local craft shop. They must have been in a huddle in the backseat, for when we hit the door they proceeded to head into a split formation to the end zone of their own predetermined location. It must have been difficult for the shopkeeper to wait on a customer whose eyes were in scanning mode during the entire transaction. Apparently, my tracking radar was on the fritz that day, for suddenly I heard my older son say, "Mom! Jake's in the paint!"

Hoping against hope, I fervently prayed I would find him just holding the bottle. Well, I was partially right—he *was* holding the bottle. Unfortunately, the contents of that bottle, a lovely beige acrylic paint, were all over the carpet of the store! It was the most horrifying, humiliating moment of my life. I vowed then never to take them anywhere together, and singly only if on a leash!

I should have foreseen my parenting future long before I did. My mother always did say, "I hope you have two kids just like you." Well, I did and now she tells me she was only kidding and didn't think I would take her that seriously. She told me once she had always thought I was a real heathen until she met my kids, and now she realizes what a great kid I really was. I have yet to determine whether she was complimenting me on my overall behavior or slamming me as a parent.

After being a parent for a few years, I found that I had developed an all-new respect for my mother. After experiencing firsthand the incredible restraint it requires not to annihilate the little darlings, I have repeatedly thanked my mother for allowing me to live to adulthood!

Chapter 4
Maternal Lies I Have Known and Loved

It seems that all mothers have a little difficulty somewhere along the line in explaining some parts of the life cycle to their children. For most, the serious trouble begins when our little darlings ask, "Where do babies come from?"

I love the old joke about the mother whose eight-year-old asks, "Where did I come from?" After a twenty-minute explanation on the reproductive cycle, the child calmly replies, "Yes, I know all that, but where was I *born?*"

There is no doubt that our children are learning about reproduction at an earlier age. As a child, I honestly believed the stork brought me; but then I also believed in Santa Claus, the Easter Bunny, and the Tooth Fairy. One by one, my heroes bit the dust—first Santa, then the Easter Bunny. By the time they nailed the Tooth Fairy, I knew my stork theory was in serious jeopardy. Once those old stand-bys had been eliminated, I began to wonder what else my parents had kept from me. ... I did not have to wait long to find the answer to that question.

Along came the lecture about the "birds and the bees." (I *still* want to know what possible correlation there is between birds, bees, and sex.) When I was twelve years old, my mother assumed I would soon be joining the ranks of womanhood. My presence was requested in Mom's bedroom. There I was handed a box marked "Kimberly-Clark." She solemnly advised me that this box would tell me everything I needed to know. Inside, I found three different types of feminine protection pads and a booklet called *You're a Young Lady Now*. After finishing this book, I had my first suspicion that womanhood was not all it was cracked up to be. The day of my first menstrual cycle coincided with the first day I ever shaved my legs. When I looked down and saw the huge amount of blood on my thigh, I was convinced I had amputated my leg ... so much for Kimberly-Clark.

Once you had acquired your monthly cycle, it became necessary for some reason to name it. Telling anyone you were "on your period" was a no-no. So while my friends and I aptly named it "the curse," my mother referred to it as "Grandma's visiting." I always rather hated that, because I never associated my grandmother's visits with such discomfort ... perhaps my dad did. Nevertheless, that is the name it assumed. Therefore, whenever I got that bloated, crampy "look-at-me-and-die" feeling we now call premenstrual syndrome (PMS), Mom would look at Dad and say, "Grandma's visiting." They would pass a knowing smile between them, and I would know I had carte blanche to be crabby for at least a week. I'm sure there were times during my adolescence that they must have thought Grandma had moved in for the duration, since I was crabby for about the next six years.

I remember during the fifth grade sitting through a very long film about male and female reproductive organs. We left that day thoroughly versed in human anatomy and physiology, without the vaguest notion of how those pesky little sperm ever got into the fallopian tubes in the first place!

Seeking additional help from my mother was only slightly more helpful. Her advice on sexual experimentation was, "Don't do it." I grew up confident in the knowledge that "nice girls don't do it before they are married." It did not take me long, however, to realize that sexual activity is not a completely black-and-white issue. There are a lot of gray areas no one tells you about. Through trial and error (some of the errors more serious than others), I finally learned sex is not just intercourse. Sex is kissing, hugging, touching, caressing, and, at last, intercourse. My mother's advice remained unchanged— "Don't do it." I found myself wondering just which part of "it" I wasn't supposed to do. Complete abstention seemed impossible at that juncture. Certain aspects of the sexual process seemed innocuous enough in and of themselves, but in combination they could become lethal in a hurry. So what's a girl to do?

Leave it to men to turn the sexual experience into a sporting event. They would advertise their sexual prowess in terms of how far they had gotten with a girl by using the baseball diamond as a map.

"Yeah," some lucky stud would proudly mutter, "got to second base with Sheila last night …"

Even girls got into the act, with whispered conversations during study hall. "Oh, Sheila! You let him get to *second* base? You *slut!*" Apparently, when a guy scored a "home run," he had won the "whole shootin' match" and was the envy of his friends for days on end. Whether or not he told the truth was hardly important.

As for me, I was never quite sure exactly what my role was in this game. Most times I felt I was just the catcher and sometimes wondered if I had ever even been up to bat. Finally I concluded that I must have been the umpire, for after calling several men "foul!" and "striking out" with others, I sometimes got to tell some of them to "take a walk" after repeated attempts at "scoring a run."

Society was not much help. I reached my somewhat premature sexual peak just in time to get hit with the propaganda from the "free love generation." According to their philosophy, sex was okey-dokey anytime, anywhere, and with anybody. Eventually it occurred to me that such higher-level thinking was fine when you were blasted out of your mind on alcohol, but it did not hold water in the light of day. Finally, we learned that "free love" was never really *free* … you always paid a price. In our day the only way sex could kill you was if your parents found out about it. Now the price of controlling sexually transmitted diseases can cost not only an arm and a leg but perhaps your life as well.

"All men want is sex." My mother and grandmother almost tattooed that on my forehead. This philosophy did seem honest enough when I was single, but it took on a whole new meaning when I finally married. Then I discovered that as soon as a man says "I do," he doesn't. For years I never got to say, "I have a headache," because he said it first! "I'm too tired" didn't enter my vocabulary until the arrival of the children. Now I know I used to like to do it, but I don't remember why!

My entire belief system has been based on some rather flawed data. I suppose it was only natural that the next institution to fall beneath the axe of reality was marriage. For most couples the phrase "happy marriage" is a contradiction in terms. One has only to look at the rising number of divorces to realize that marriage is definitely not for sissies.

It takes a lot of courage to stay in a difficult marriage. It is hard to stay when your feet, head, and heart say, "Go, go, go!" It takes more than hearts, flowers, and a lovely wedding to ensure that a marriage that will stand the test of time. Marriage takes a lot of work—it is like a job. We don't become adept at our jobs overnight. It takes several years of experience to really feel comfortable and confident.

The eminent surgeon does not become so overnight. It takes years of study, preparation, and practical application before his or her profession becomes established. Why do you think they call it "practicing medicine"? They have to practice until they get it right! Yet we look at the equally challenging job of marriage and expect it to reach perfection immediately. In a world that values disposable items, marriage has become equally expendable. "Until divorce do us part" has become preferable to the original contract agreement. Had my husband and I filed for divorce every time we felt the marriage was a failure, they would have needed a revolving door on the courthouse!

I do not mean to imply that my husband and I will never see divorce or separation. We have often privately joked that the only reason we are still together is that neither one of us wants to deal with the kids 24/7, 365 without a backup plan! In all honesty, my husband and I love our children without question and beyond measure. However, our desire not to be single parents is superseded only by our desire not to die of a lengthy, debilitating disease!

Some evenings I meet my husband at the door with red-rimmed eyes, near hysteria, screaming, "*You* take them for awhile—I'm *outta* here!" Honestly, if it weren't for his backup support, I am absolutely certain my white uniforms would have been replaced by white straitjackets long before now. My husband knows without question that the best way to send me into a state of apoplexy is the mere mention of a third child. Just the word *pregnant* would send me scampering into the bathroom to double-check the expiration date on my birth control pills.

I did not enjoy pregnancy, despite the fact that I really wanted to. All my life I had woven intricate fantasies about the marvel of carrying the child of the man I loved. But you have to admit it is hard to be enthusiastic about a process that leaves you "driving the porcelain bus" for months. They say a pregnant woman "glows." Well, the only thing that glowed about this pregnant woman was my hemorrhoids, and those babies glowed in the dark!

I was one of those unfortunate women who by necessity are into maternity clothes approximately eight minutes after conception. Nearly two years postpartum I continued to wage an all-out war with the "battle of the bulge." My husband refers to parts of my old wardrobe as my "coaster collection," for, as he says, "That is all you'll ever be able to use them for again." Friends who haven't seen me for awhile ask if I'm pregnant again … I tell them it's gas.

After taking the standard Lamaze class, I felt prepared to achieve "natural" childbirth. After living through two experiences, I am convinced that this term *had* to have come from a male. Any woman can tell you there is absolutely nothing natural about expelling a watermelon through a four-inch opening, which is the best way I can describe the labor process.

Men are usually less than understanding about the degree of pain the woman experiences. While trying to deliver a 9 pound 2 ½ ounce baby, my doctor looked calmly over his surgical mask and announced, "Now, Jan, you can't have a baby without a little pain." I politely informed him that I had passed "a little pain" about three hours prior. I still believe that had I been able to get my leg out of the stirrups, a well-placed kick in the appropriate location might have enlightened the good doctor as to the exact extent of my discomfort!

They say a woman forgets all about the pain once the baby arrives. I do not totally agree with that philosophy. It has been years since my last pregnancy, and I still remember enough to know I'd prefer not to repeat the effort.

Despite my bluster about the ills of pregnancy, there truly were some marvelous moments that defy explanation. The early feelings of movement exceeded my wildest dreams. There is a tremendous sense of humility knowing that a little life is so dependent on you for survival.

In the 1970s I joined protestors who believed that abortion should be a woman's choice. It wasn't until I did a surgical rotation through the abortion clinic and saw what we do to babies in the name of women's "rights" that I realized that my "rights" would come at the expense of some terrible wrongs. There is no question in my mind that life begins at the moment of conception. Simple reasoning tells us there can be no cell division without life. How, then, can we argue we are not killing babies? It would seem the whole question centers around viability. When does one determine when a baby is real?

My baby became real for me the moment I knew of its existence. A rosebud picked before its time is still a flower. As I look at my younger son and his dimpled face smiles back at me, it is hard for me to believe I could have chosen not to have him. That cute little blond-haired boy could have ended up as a pile of biohazardous material dumped in with other human refuse. It seems wrong to me now for anyone to have that much power.

I had concluded there may be another reason why some women forget the pain of childbirth. It is because they are too busy to think about it. The fear of childbirth is quickly replaced by the fear of having a newborn in the house. I remember feeling quite unnerved by the presence of that little alien in the front bedroom. I refer to my oldest son as an alien because due to difficulty in delivering him, he was forcibly removed with a device called a Mityvac. (We thought briefly of naming him Hoover, since he was literally vacuumed out!) The pressure applied to the head to pull him out caused it to become somewhat misshapen, rather cone-shaped. I also refer to my son as an alien because I didn't feel for him what I thought I should. I assumed the "mother instinct" would just kick in, and I would know just what to do. Wrong answer. I was told that a mother soon learns to interpret the meaning of her child's cry, that each cry sounds different. I am here to tell you they still sound the same to me. Sometimes I couldn't even understand what my four-year-old was crying about, and he could talk! I am only just now beginning to appreciate my kids, reveling in their triumphs and commiserating in their failures.

I was a late bloomer, having my first child at age thirty. I thought that once they cut the umbilical cord, we were freed from each other, but I have learned that an invisible umbilical cord binds you forever. I read somewhere that a mother fights to be free from the constraints of her children almost as much as they fight to gain independence from her. With all that fighting going on, it is a wonder we ever find time to build a relationship!

My mother-in-law says that you never quit worrying about your kids. I am about to decide that she is quite right. Even when I put six states between me and them, they were always right there with me, never leaving me for a minute. I hope I am that lucky when I am old!

**"This is the perfect watch for mothers.
Every day is 36 hours!"**

Chapter 5
That Elusive "Quality Time"

Well, here you are … the house is clean, the yard is mowed, the bills are paid, and the laundry is caught up (a situation that will last approximately ten minutes). It is now time for "quality time with the children." So now that you have the time, what do you do with them?

As parents we strive to assure our children a happy childhood by purchasing whatever the television tells our children they cannot live without. Television has been called "America's Ultimate Babysitter." I am constantly amazed by the amount of junk that is offered to today's kids and how advertising hype would make these things seem impossible to do without.

At one time my son believed that the Teenage Mutant Ninja Turtles were the only toy worth possessing. Dragging me into the family room one day, he breathlessly informed me that he needed a Flush-O-Matic Torture Device for his turtles. I sat transfixed before the TV and watched a plastic turtle lying complacently on a table while a child poured horrible green gooey stuff on his face. I had just spent fifty dollars to have the plumber rectify a similar situation in the bathroom. If I had known it was so important, I could have given him his own Flush-O-Matic Torture Device for real, for *free*!

In recalling my childhood, it is not the big things my parents and grandparents did or bought for me that stand out in my mind. Rather, it is the small things that I remember, like Grandma making a tent by pitching a blanket over the clothesline, or Mom letting us wear her old prom dresses to liven up a tea party. I remember once when Mom brought out a tray with ice cream and Coke floats for me and my friends, actually serving them to us. I tell you, no waiter in a fancy restaurant could surpass the memory of my mother on that day.

Perhaps what I enjoyed most about my mother was how easily she could be distracted. One day my friends and I were playing a game called Tickle Bee. It was a simple game, involving leading a plastic-coated metal bug around curved trails with a magnet. We taught her how to play the game, and she became so engrossed that she forgot she had left the water faucet running in the kitchen sink. When the water began leaking out of the front door, our "quality time with Mom" came to an abrupt halt.

I suppose that part of my lack of preparedness for parenting stems from the fact that I am an only child. Having no sibling experience, I am continually amazed at how many things my children can find to fight over and about. Despite the fact that their closet could pass as an outlet store for Toys-R-Us, they always seem to want the same toy at the same time. The only thing I have to compare it to would be early marriage, when you discover that nothing you own is ever sacred again.

I have spent countless nights tossing and turning, worrying whether I am teaching my children enough. In a country where three-year-olds know the alphabet, I am extremely aware that they are going to have a lot of competition. Where does one find the balance between too much and not enough? Teach them too much and they are bored in school. Teach them too little and the only cap they will ever wear is the one marked *Dunce*.

It is my firm belief that in the end, it will not be the trips to Disney World or the big bicycle I bought for my kids that they will recall in later years. It may be some silly, insignificant thing I may not even remember I did, because I was busy doing something else. This just proves to me that I need to live each day like it is the most important one of my life, for it may be during a simple day that I will do something that my children will recall as a favorite memory.

Parents do the best they can with what they have to give. It is easy to blame our parents for our faults and shortcomings, but it isn't until you become one that you truly appreciate the effort that goes into it. Thanks, Mom … and Dad!

Chapter 6
The Way to a Man's Heart

They say the way to a man's heart is through his stomach. Personally, I hope there is an alternate route.

I am a lousy cook. My culinary disgrace is legendary. One of my dearest friends immortalized my inability with an apron that says "Betty the Crock." Now you might think this an unkind thing for a friend to do, but I like to think of it as our way to laugh at the kitchen faux pas we all make. I happen to know for a fact that she has a recipe for "armor-coated fish" that could break a denture plate at fifty feet.

My ineptitude is not for lack of material. You will usually find a food calendar from a women's magazine taped to my refrigerator door. My kitchen cabinets sport one whole cabinet full of cookbooks and recipe cards. But despite all that expert advice, my recipe classics include "Salmonella Soufflé" and "Ptomaine Tortillas."

My husband told me when we married that he was a basic meat-and-potatoes kind of guy. It took me a while to figure out that this means he wants potato chips at every meal. But I get bored with the same old menus. I will find a sumptuous, mouth-watering recipe in a magazine. I rush home, armed to the teeth with every possible ingredient, and spend the whole day slaving away over a hot microwave.

But no matter how I try to faithfully reproduce that tasty jewel, it never looks (or I suspect tastes) like what's pictured. It is enough to make me crazy. Presenting my new find to the family usually results in the same scenario; the husband and children wrinkle their noses in disgust and gravely inquire, "What *was* it?" Even the dog won't eat it. Tired and distraught, I trundle back to the kitchen to whip up hamburgers and french fries, which in my state of dejection I usually burn. I have spent many dollars and many nights weeping softly while dumping a new recipe in the garbage. I feel righteously indignant about the "swine" in my home who wouldn't know taste if it bit them.

I believe my culinary inability was genetically inherited. I think my mom hated to cook. Her recipe file included "stuffed hot dogs" and Kraft macaroni and cheese. Her emphasis for me during my childhood was to teach me to dust the furniture … something she hated more than cooking. I could not wait to have daughters so I could palm off the dusting on them. Do you find it at all ironic that I had two sons?

I have devoted my life to answering the dilemma of how I can spend a hundred dollars or more a week on groceries, yet there is still nothing to eat. Searching for a late-evening goodie usually results in severe depression. "What do we have to eat that's *edible?*" is the standard question each evening. I suppose it is a fair question. Coming from a family where money was tight, I learned to do some pretty creative things with leftovers. For example, leftover mashed potatoes became potato casseroles or stuffed hot dogs. Stale bread became stuffing. Then I discovered the joy of homemade vegetable soup, learning that leftover vegetables could be saved for days, then magically become soup. The only problem is, by the time I remember to make the soup, I usually find fuzzy stuff on at least part of the vegetables. My husband refuses to eat anything in the refrigerator unless I am there to verify the longevity of any given item. He once told me he was only sorry Sir Alexander Fleming had already discovered penicillin, because he could have made a fortune on the stuff in our refrigerator!

My husband has already genetically passed his delicate palate on to his sons. I had difficulty seeing the physical resemblance between my husband and his sons when they were first born. Then one day they curled up their little noses and simultaneously asked, "What's *this* stuff?" The resemblance to their father was unmistakable.

They say a son grows up believing no one can cook like his mother. I hope for *my* sons' sakes it is true. Can't you just *hear* it? "Gee, honey, you just don't burn 'em the way Mom can!"

Snack time has become my deepest nightmare. The mother truly committed to nutrition just cannot condone the "Hostess Ho-Ho Diet" that my children subscribe to. My children's concept of "lovin' from the oven" truly does have Pillsbury written all over it. Honestly, I have tried, though. Children's magazines are full of snappy little snack ideas that supposedly even a child can do. What they don't tell you is that these same children also have names like Einstein and Edison. It becomes just another example of "looks like an ice cream clown in the magazine—looks like a doggy yard-deposit in reality." After all, my children can open the child-proof bottles when I can't. They were afflicted with a mother who can take the simple sewing pattern marked "Make It Tonight" and spend two weeks working on it.

I even sent surveys to American women across the county and asked for creative snack ideas. This was because this book originally was an attempt to see how we as modern women could somehow bring forward some of the best concepts from the decades that preceded us. Apparently, most of the women I surveyed have also come up with the dumpy ice cream clown, because the top contenders for *healthy* snacks were as follows:

Popcorn	Fresh fruit with dip
Fresh-baked breads	Fresh vegetables with dip
Cookies—all kinds	Anything with dip
Iced graham crackers	Peanut butter and jelly sandwiches
Jell-O	Popsicles

There was one enterprising woman who shared a recipe with pears, cream cheese, and pecan pieces. Theoretically, one is supposed to roll the cream cheese into little balls, place it in the pear halves, and sprinkle pecan pieces over the top. I do have a few questions about this recipe. You see, I tried this recipe with canned pears, and they were such slippery devils that I kept shooting them across the kitchen. Furthermore, I had cream cheese up to my elbows trying to make the little balls. My hands got so sticky that the pecan pieces clung to my hands. Finally, I resorted to just licking the mixture off my hands and serving plain pears (after I cleaned the fur-balls off of them, of course).

There was another recipe that called for taking a slice out of an apple, spreading peanut butter on the sliced-out areas and placing marshmallows across the front. When completed it is supposed to resemble an open mouth with teeth. The dog barked at it during the entire meal, later stole it off the table, and buried it in the backyard to make sure it was quite dead.

My quest to find healthy snacks for my children was further thwarted by learning to read the food label. For the longest time I didn't have a clue what was in the food I was eating, because most of it was in some kind of code. Later, when I did a little more research, I found that most of these names were additives and preservatives. By the time I took into consideration the fat content, the amount of sugar, and the additives and preservatives, it appeared there was very little nutritional value to anything I planned to serve!

My son has Attention Deficit Disorder, and while the experts say there is no link between diet and A.D.D., I heartily disagree. I know exactly when my son has had a regular Coke with caffeine, because his hyperactivity increases tenfold! In fact, whenever I relent and allow a "regular" diet, comprised of sugared cereals, snacks with high-fructose corn syrup, etc., I can expect him to climb the walls.

My younger son has a number of food allergies, including milk and Red Dye #40. It is utterly amazing how many foods contain this dye! I can always tell when he has had either one, because his ears turn flaming red and are warm to the touch. He has learned that this is an uncomfortable sensation and generally tries to avoid foods that contain these substances. One waitress in a local eating establishment was alternately stunned and amused when my five-year-old son inquired whether a certain entrée contained Red Dye #40.

When working with heart patients, I tell them, "You are what you eat ... if you eat fat, then you will *be* fat!" Statistics show that this generation's kids are ten to twelve pounds heavier than the generation that preceded them. This fact is attributed to increased television viewing and prolonged playing of video games instead of engaging in active cardiovascular exercise. Cardiovascular disease is showing up at earlier and earlier ages. With the high cost and uncertainty about the state of health care in America, it would seem that the best gift we moms can give our children is to educate them (and ourselves) about the process of fueling the human engine!

If the way to a man's heart is truly through his stomach, I suppose it is my job to take the safest route there. We now serve "reduced-fat" potato chips at every meal. ... Oh, well. Rome wasn't built in a day!

"I need to simplify my life. Bring home a bag
of dog chow, cat chow, kid chow and parent chow."

Chapter 7
Vacationing with Children— A Contradiction in Terms!

I have come to the strong conclusion that there is no such thing as a "family vacation." Generally speaking; either you have a family or you have a vacation; they are mutually exclusive. In the old days (BC), I remember, there were relaxing walks on the beach, lingering hours in restaurants and lounges, and trips to museums and amusement parks where you actually saw the sights you went there to see.

Vacations have now fallen into the category of "same stuff, different location." In getting ready for vacationing with children, you must prepare for every potential problem, every potential disaster. If you don't take at least ten outfits per child per day, you will run out of clothes. If you don't take everything in the medicine cabinet, you will be out driving around at three o'clock in the morning looking for an all-night convenience store that sells cough medicine.

Traveling with infants and toddlers is the ultimate nightmare. The first trip in a two-door car with an infant was a real eye-opener. By the time all the appropriate paraphernalia was loaded, we could barely find the baby. We discovered the best way to locate him was to wait until he started crying and then track the sound of his wailing until we found him. This sent us screaming to the nearest car lot for a minivan. Owning a minivan allowed us to carry everything but the kitchen sink. Then we discovered the cartop carrier. This enabled us to get the kitchen sink in also.

I have learned an invaluable lesson about the intricacies of traveling with a cartop carrier. Most important, I learned you do not try to drive into the garage after attaching the car-top carrier to the van. Yes sir, there we were, running around doing errands, preparing to leave for a family vacation. For whatever reason, I opted to pull into the garage, forgetting all about the little gadget on the top. I hit the driveway at cruising altitude and was halfway into the garage when I heard a thump, and the van came to an abrupt stop. I rapidly noted that my foot was nowhere near the brake. I hurriedly tried to pull back out, but to no avail. I tried to pull forward but couldn't do that either. Still feeling confident I had the situation under control, I got out to survey the damage. I was horrified to discover that I had neatly created a V-shaped dent in the carrier, wedging it tightly around the garage door. Short of a miracle, I was in deep trouble.

That evening my husband and three of his friends let all the air out of the tires and used their combined weights to create enough downward pressure to dislodge the wedged van from what I had feared was its permanent resting place. Standing at the back door, I was privy to their vaguely amusing unanimous decision that I had won the award for "Dumb Wife Trick of the Year."

Living in a small town does not help. By the next morning, everyone in town had heard of my minor miscalculation, and everyone but I found it hilarious. I thought that by the time we returned from a ten-day trip, the story would be old history. Instead the story had become legendary. I was welcomed home with greetings of "Hey, how about that cartop carrier?" Even now, years later, when the neighbors hear we are going on vacation, they all want to know if the cartop carrier will be joining us. One year I found my next-door neighbor parked in a lawn chair in the side yard facing the garage door. When I questioned him about his choice of location, he laughingly told me he'd heard we were leaving that morning, and he didn't want to miss the show!

I have found that the only thing worse than doing something really stupid once is repeating the effort. Some years later we took a joint vacation with my husband's best friend and his children. In fact, vacationing with "Uncle Roski" has become a family tradition. We made a trip to Myrtle Beach in South Carolina. It was a beautiful place. The first night we had dinner out, and Roski's son took his car out to "cruise the chicks." The following morning we heard raised voices and were informed that the son had encountered car trouble and had just left the car and walked home. Unfortunately, he didn't have a clue which street he had left it on. So my husband and Uncle Roski spent the morning finding the car, then taking it to the repair shop to have the alternator repaired. We teased the kid all morning about this great start to the vacation. When the men returned I took our older son out souvenir shopping, as promised. Leaving the parking garage, my son confidently assured me, "There's the exit." Well, indeed we had used this exit the night before when we had gone to dinner. However, we had gone to dinner in Roski's car. We were now in the *van,* and this exit did not accommodate a van with a cartop carrier!

We spent the next hour in the parking lot facing the beach, with me lying inside the badly dented cartop carrier still attached to the roof of the van, trying to kick the dents out enough to get it closed. I was not successful. I tried to prepare my son for the tirade I knew was to follow. All the way up in the elevator, I coached him.

"Now," I sternly admonished him, "*I* will tell your father. You just keep your mouth shut."

"Okay, Mom," he said, "I understand."

Right before we entered the room, I repeated my warning.

"I'm not kidding, Nick. If you want to see your next birthday, you'll let me handle this!"

35

"Okay, Mom," he said, "no problem!"

We opened the door to the hotel room, and he immediately shouted, *"Hey, Dad! Guess who just ripped the cartop carrier off the van again!"*

You can imagine the rest of the scene.

While vacations were once associated with rest and relaxation, they are now based on where we can take the children where they will do the least damage. This usually includes a steady diet of McDonald's foods, and frequent hunts for rest areas and gas stations. And then there is the inevitable question that always comes five minutes into a ten-hour trip: "Are we there yet?"

From our experience, we also learned that Disney World is lost on the very young. When our oldest son was two and half, we unloaded a fortune to stay inside the park for three days. While there he contracted an ear infection and was totally unimpressed with the Magic Kingdom. He was, however, completely fascinated with the baby pool and the revolving door into the lobby of the hotel.

I also hold the firm belief that children are nature's way of sabotaging every adult attempt at regaining sanity. Consider if you will their innate ability to become ill at the mere mention of the word *vacation.* I believe children come equipped with an inborn radar that zeroes in on their immune system, causing it to malfunction about two to five hours before their parents' estimated time of departure.

I base this theory on an attempt at a getaway that henceforth shall be named the "Vacation from Hell." We had planned weeks in advance for a five-day trip to Tennessee over a holiday weekend and were scheduled to leave after work. My first feeling of impending doom came when the babysitter called me at work and informed me that I had a sick child. Having dealt with a doctor who barely spoke English at a Florida urgent care center (also known as a "doc in a box") on our last vacation, I immediately rushed the boy to our family physician. Reassured by his diagnosis of "just a little fluid behind the ear," and armed to the teeth with antibiotics, cough syrup, Tylenol, antihistamines, decongestants, and Benadryl, we proceeded on schedule. Those first twelve hours were sheer bliss.

The first full day dawned clear and bright. We shared a leisurely breakfast, then prepared for a final bathroom stop before taking off. Placing my toddler on the floor, I turned to wipe the crumbs from the high chair. Instead of crumbs, I found a rather large mass of semiliquid poop. Gazing at it, first with incomprehension, then with dawning horror, I visually tracked the source to my son's backside. Alarmingly, this association was made simultaneous with my son's decision to plop the aforementioned backside firmly beside a table of happy diners who had just acquired their breakfast.

In a blinding flash of light (and a trail of yellow poop), the child was whisked from the dining room. I am certain that All-American football player George Gipp (a famous Notre Dame running back from 1917 to 1920) could not have covered yardage any quicker. Since all the clothes were in the infamous cartop carrier, a quick stop at Kmart for a new wardrobe seemed the logical second stop.

By afternoon, we were confident the worst was behind us. So confident were we that we decided to stop at Mammoth Cave. Approximately 250 feet underground, Mr. Diarrhea Man came forth with round two. While the quantity was smaller, its aroma was no less pungent.

Morning two can only be described as tentative. My older son's lack of appetite was met with the usually parental admonishment: "Eat your breakfast!" He did and then promptly proceeded to heave it all back into his scrambled eggs. While carrying the second child in what had become a comfortable football hold, it occurred to me that if motherhood didn't work out, I might have my own brilliant career as a football running back.

The day deteriorated rapidly. Gradually, at half-day intervals, everyone in our party, including a friend from Chicago, contracted the virus. We had enticed her to join us, promising her "the weekend of your dreams." It certainly was, but of the nightmare variety!

Home again once more, I contemplated the fact while unpacking that the sum total of the souvenirs from our minivacation included seven empty bottles of Gatorade, a six-pack of 7-Up, and a half-empty bottle of antidiarrhea medicine.

Oh well, there's always next year ...

Chapter 8
The Ultimate Reason That Dogs Are *Man's* Best Friend

The ultimate reason why dogs are man's best friend is because men usually bring them home, and women get stuck taking care of them.

Our family must have the words "Suckers Live Here" emblazoned across the door in an invisible flashing neon sign, for every stray dog and cat in town ends up on our doorstep. We do not require a pedigree for admission to our petting zoo; any old mutt will do. We have a wider variety of pets than the Humane Society.

We had a goldfish named Monsieur Pesky. He was found floating belly up one morning and was subsequently buried in the backyard. Next came a parakeet; he did not last long enough to name. He was eaten one day by the cat and was also subsequently buried in the backyard. Unfortunately, while finding the perfect final resting place for the bird, we unearthed Monsieur Pesky. This just proves my theory that there is not a peaceful moment at our house—alive *or* dead!

We never get the Lassies or Rin-Tin-Tins of this world. We get dogs like Berle Speedwagon, who chewed the claw feet off of our antique dining room table. We get dogs like Yogi, who was so named for his resemblance in size and appearance to a big black bear. His penchant was for dropping ticks on my carpet. He was also a nomad, wandering from yard to yard, a fact that thrilled my neighbors to death.

But the one who nearly drove me to complete mental collapse was a dog named Mildred. I was more than eight months pregnant when my husband brought home a poor bedraggled and *ugly* dog. Mildred looked like she must have had at least fourteen fathers. To her credit she was a warm, loving dog who just happened to be filled to overflowing with a belly full of puppies. She looked so uncomfortable and, being so pregnant myself, I could not bring myself to put her out in the winter cold. That was my first mistake. Mildred burrowed in for a long winter's nap at the foot of our bed. She also delivered her puppies there … on our new carpet.

Obviously, the foot of our bed was no place for a family of eight, so they moved to the nearby living room. For the next six weeks, I listened to the very loud, and progressively irritating, sound of their suckling. Just when I thought I would go crazy, they started barking. Actually, it was more of a high-pitched yapping. I was thrilled when I finally went into labor and could leave the house for some long-overdue sleep at the hospital.

When I returned home, I discovered they had learned how to sing seven-part harmony, at decibels loud enough to rouse both Monsieur Pesky and the parakeet. I don't need to tell you that the combination of a three-year-old son, a screaming newborn, seven yapping puppies, three adult dogs, three cats, and a postpartum mother with raging hormones was not a pretty picture!

The puppies moved to the laundry room, from which they soon learned to escape. I came home to find six dozen piles and puddles. It was just too much. They moved to the garage or the yard; the latter soon rivaled Minnesota, Land of 10,000 Lakes, after their discovery of hole digging as an art form.

Eventually, we found homes for all the puppies, but not before spending a fortune on puppy vaccinations and puppy chow. I even threw in a four-pound bag of puppy food with each free puppy that left the huddle.

The problem was Mildred. I don't know whether she was angry about the unsolicited adoption of her babies or if she was latently psychotic, but she developed a penchant for trashing the house. Left alone in the house, she would demolish it, going even so far as to chew the crotch out of my underwear! She would also dig crater-sized holes in the yard, chew up the kids' toys, and unearth my hybrid iris. In the garage, she would demolish the cat litter boxes, shred newspapers, and poop everywhere. She seemed to zero in on things belonging to the kids and me, rarely destroying things belonging to my husband. I think he believed I was exaggerating, right up until she chewed the covers off the stereo speakers. It was then, at last, time to unload Mildred.

But who was going to take a psychotic ugly dog? The answer came like a miracle during my summer garage sale. A young man looking for bargains remarked how unusual Mildred was. Sensing an answer to prayer, I immediately asked, "Would you like to have her?" When he said yes, I flew into the house like a flash to get her proof of spaying, immunization records, and complimentary dog food. I was overjoyed!

I must admit a moment of true remorse when, while loading the dog into the car, I noticed the man's wife was very pregnant. However, to feel guilty is one thing; to miss an opportunity to unload that dog, quite another. Good-bye, Mildred—and good luck!

The most recent acquisition is a mutt called Red Ryder. He dropped by our house last Labor Day weekend and just forgot to leave. He is another dog who is so ugly that he's rather cute. His physical appearance, however, is where the resemblance to cute ends. He has some really disgusting habits, like chasing cars and kids on bikes. I hate having outdoor dogs, but I'll make an exception in his case. He just can't decide whether he wants to be to be an indoor or outdoor dog, although he seems to prefer being an indoor dog just after romping in the creek, with mud to his haunches, or after rolling in something quite dead. When he is the dirtiest or the smelliest is when he is adamant about being a lapdog.

He also has a deep and abiding love for chew bones, and if one is not available, the back of a couch or the side of a recliner will do just fine. We have found he has a rather sensitive palate, in that most dry dog foods do not appeal to him. However, cat food cans from the neighbors' houses, and carcasses of animals, seem to appeal to him immediately. I looked out in the side yard one day to find eight empty cat food cans, one dead cat, two deer legs (what happened to the *rest* of it?), and what might have at one time been a beaver or muskrat. I was horrified, but Ryder seemed perfectly content, lying in a three-foot deep crater he had freshly dug in the yard. To give him his due, he is good at unearthing moles … which in our yard will become a full-time profession.

Living with Red Ryder has had its more humorous moments. One day while my husband was taking his morning walk on the treadmill, Ryder came in to investigate the noise. He peered with great interest at my husband and then hopped up to join him. The dog shot right between my husband's legs and landed face first in the laundry basket! The next day he came in while I was walking on the treadmill, curled his lip, growled at us both, and walked out of the bedroom.

The cats are only slightly less trouble. I can usually locate them by following their trail of regurgitated hairballs or "pieces" from their latest quest for wild game.

When you have more than one pet, someone is always either wanting to go outside or waiting to come inside. We thought we had solved the problem by installing a cat door, so that they could let themselves in and out at their leisure. What we did not count on was the fact they would bring their friends in with them. One night I woke up to the sound of banging and crashing. Terrified we were being robbed, I tiptoed out to discover two cats, each with field mice, playing volleyball with their prey.

My husband usually has little to say about the pet antics. Except, of course, on the day of the "Great Mole Escapade." One day I discovered the kitties had brought a live mole into my bedroom. Having never seen one before, I marveled at how soft their fur really is. Then it occurred to me that unless I wanted to add a mole to the menagerie, I had to get him out of the house fast. I did what seemed at the time a very rational thing; I put him in a bucket and carried him outside.

A few days later my husband came into the house with a determined look on his face. He asked what I had done with the mole. When I told him, I honestly thought he was going to cry.

"You put a burrowing mole in the side yard where I planted the new grass seed?" he wailed. I stepped outside to find that indeed the pesky little critter had burrowed trails all over the yard. Live and learn!

I simply cannot understand why pets cannot be included on the family insurance plan. Their vaccinations and surgeries are often as expensive as their human counterparts', but generally without the ability to recoup the loss. I have spent a king's ransom for heartworm pills, flea allergy shots, pills, spraying, and flea collars, and the darned dog still has the audacity to spread my garbage all over the kitchen floor.

Another thing I cannot understand is why dogs feel the need to nibble on the little "kitty cigars" in the litter box. I had one dog that forever had a little cheroot hanging from her mouth. She looked like a gangster. I was concerned the dog was suffering from a nutritional deficiency. The veterinarian, however, assured me she was perfectly normal and that yard delicacies are the dog's version of chocolates. I just don't understand that—yard chocolates don't even have nuts. Personally, I would prefer to just buy the dog a box of Fannie Mae— the doggie kisses afterward would definitely be easier to tolerate!

Chapter 9
All Stressed Up and Nowhere to Go

No one will ever say that I was a paragon of virtue or had a wealth of patience. I am more than likely when provoked to tell you just what I am thinking, in no uncertain terms. It is one of the few vices I cling to with a passion.

Most of my favorite stress relievers are unhealthy or fattening. When I developed asthma I gave up cigarettes. When I developed ulcers I gave up alcohol. I used to enjoy a sleazy novel from time to time, but now, if I find the time to read, I feel guilty knowing I am filling my mind with useless tripe when I should be reading books on how to raise difficult children or to be a better Christian. When I started having kids, it seems I lost myself somewhere along the way.

I used to find it inconceivable that a man could walk out on his wife and family. How could he just abandon the wife and kids who love him? Then I realized that most men figure they could be gone a week before anyone would miss them.

Even in our humdrum existence our schedules are so hectic that my husband and I barely see each other. Our primary topic of communication is who will be picking up the kids from the babysitter's house. If I want to know what my husband is doing, I usually can find out by reading the community newspaper. He is very community-minded, which basically means he gets stuck doing most of the jobs no one else wants to do.

The other way I communicate with my husband is via our friends. That is usually how I keep up with my social calendar as well. "Hey," my friends will tell me, "did you know we are going out for dinner on Saturday night?" My babysitter is often given a frantic last-minute call. Thank goodness she is a flexible person.

Anytime my husband and I try to carry on an adult conversation, it is usually punctuated by "Hey, Mom!" or "Hey, Dad!" A simple five-minute conversation takes fifteen minutes, and when it is over we barely remember what we were talking about.

I am a sucker for "how-to" articles in ladies' magazines. Titles like "How to Rev Up Your Marriage," and "How to Put the Spark Back in Your Husband's Battery" can entice me quicker than the *National Inquirer* headlines. All of them insist that time alone together is a must, but they don't tell you how to achieve that minor miracle. My parents and in-laws work all week—the last thing they want is to spend a weekend corralling kids. After all, they already raised their kids, right? Besides that, if you and your husband are out working all week, how can you justify leaving the kids again for romantic junket for two?

I have elaborate fantasies of kidnapping my husband and heading for the nearest "no-tell motel" for a weekend of passionate lust. So far a fantasy is all it is. I am living for the day when my kids are old enough to develop friends who want them to stay overnight. The first weekend they are both out for the night, I plan to whip out my collection of "how-to" articles, and then—*look out, babycakes, here I come!* I can only hope he is still around when that happens. My mother tries to console me by saying, "Have patience, dear, your time will come." I wonder if I will still look good in a teddy when I am sixty-five!

There are plenty of things in the adult world to supply us with an endless amount of stress. Aside from the usual stresses that television commercials illustrate for us, there are the million and one other aggravations. I have concluded that it will not be the big things that will push me over the edge, but rather one little insignificant thing that will gently nudge me into the abyss.

Every year at the beginning of school, we are assaulted from all sides from organizations of all kinds, all trying to raise money. Now, please do not misunderstand; I feel that many of the organizations are truly worthwhile causes, but suddenly every time you answer the door, there stand the Boy Scouts, the Girl Scouts, the high school band, the Little League, the elementary- and middle-school fund-raisers ... the list is endless. I dread to answer the door anymore. I have seriously considered coming up with a device not unlike the telephone answering machine that will work on the front door. "I'm sorry," the machine will say. "No one can answer the door at this time. If you will state the purpose of your visit, someone will either answer the door or get back with you. Thank you."

Finally I make it past the little fund-raisers who magically seem to appear every time I go out the front door. Thinking I have at last found a little peace and quiet, the mother of some little fund-raiser sneaks up on me when I am not looking, to tell me that her son is selling ...

If *he* is selling the stuff, why am I buying it from *her?* I have enough coffee mugs to open a coffee shop, enough sausage and cheese to open a deli, and enough candles to start the second Great Chicago Fire! I have tried selling this stuff in garage sales, but I cannot move it because everyone else is trying to sell theirs! I have even considered taking this stuff and hitting the road with my own show. How about "Send a Mom to Sanity Camp"? I am pretty sure a week in Tahiti could cure whatever ails me.

What I want to know is why these organizations don't come up with something we can use. If they have to sell something, why not a gift certificate to a favorite restaurant, or a promise to babysit for one evening for each twenty-dollar donation? Or better yet, wouldn't it be easier to just give the kids a flat donation? Then the five or ten dollars you give would go solely to the item they are trying to raise the money for. Instead of trying to figure out what to do with all the junk, we could just take a nice tax deduction for charitable donations. Do you think I could run for Congress on that platform?

Life has become entirely too complicated. Remember when you were a kid and your friend had something that belonged to you? As I recall, the situation was handled in one of two ways:

1. You negotiated a deal, or
2. You beat the crud out of each other until someone walked away with the prize.

Now, either way, you handled the problem on a one-on-one basis, and the situation was resolved in a timely manner and did not cost a lot of money, aside from the cost of the stitches in your face, that is. Now our political squabbles involve multiple parties, including millions of individuals who sometimes aren't even sure what the squabble is all about. Instead of resolving an argument in a day, we drag it out for months and years and spend billions of dollars we don't have to resolve the situation. Wouldn't it make more sense to send the heads of the nations involved into the ring to just duke it out?

If the country's checkbook is in the red, we call it the national debt. If my bank account is in the red, we call it bankruptcy. If our country is indeed supposed to be "of the people, by the people, for the people," then does that mean we are all broke? If someone perpetually borrows money from you and never pays it back, don't you begin to lose respect for him? If so, then how can we as Americans legitimately pride ourselves on our integrity? Personally, I would favor a five-year freeze on government spending. Then if each man, woman, and child in the country paid a hundred dollars a year, it seems to me, we could at least put a dent into the payment of the national debt. At least it would look like we are trying, and that has to count for something.

My most brilliant brainstorm is that male heads of state should retire for one year and let their wives or mothers take over. I'm willing to bet wars would come to an end. What woman in her right mind would voluntarily send her son out in a minefield to play? I can just see this scenario:

"No, Mr. President, you can't go out and play with the Soviets until you clean up your economy."

"But, Mommm! I want to buy some new F-14s!"

"I told you before, son. Until you learn to take care of what you already have, I am *not* buying you anything else!"

I cannot imagine any woman going through pregnancy, labor, childbirth, colic, teething, the "terrible twos," midnight illnesses, braces, Little League practices and games, adolescence, and the myriad of other child-rearing bonuses, only to lose that child to war or other forms of violence. My heart goes out to any parent that I hear of who must undergo such tragedy.

Stress has become the key word in the vocabulary of today's family. I watch Kim, my partner at work, as she examines her personal schedule to find a free night to spend at home. It seems every night is filled with meetings, sporting events with the children, and countless activities that keep them away from the very family time they are striving for.

My schedule often looks like this, too. The only difference between Kim and me is that I no longer enjoy the hustle-bustle. For several years therapists and my family physician admonished me, saying that I needed to slow down and take time for myself, but I didn't seem to know how. Then, finally, when a nervous breakdown seemed imminent, I began to relinquish some of my activities. I really believed everything would fall apart without me, but fortunately (or unfortunately), life seemed to go on without a hitch. Kim once said,

"If you want to know how important you are in this life, throw a rock in a pond. It does create a ripple for a second, but then the water smoothes out, and you'll never know the rock was even there."

I found this thought horribly depressing at first, but gradually I began to drop out from one organization and then another. After the first few weeks of missing the feeling that I was in the middle of things, I began to relax. Now it seems I have gone the other direction and resent everything that takes me away from home. I can't decide whether I need a new job or if this is what a midlife crisis is about … all stressed up and nowhere to go.

Chapter 10
"I Can't Believe I Said That!" The Day I Fell into the Generation Gap

As a kid I once vowed, "I am *never* going to say that to my kids!" I recently spouted off an oft-used "Mom-ism" to my kids and then clamped my hands over my mouth in total disbelief that I had really said that ... another great illusion shot to heck.

Apparently, all mothers resort to "Mom-isms"—those little sayings that seem to go in one ear and out the other. Fortunately, some of the better ones manage to stay between our ears and eventually skip out of our own mouths. I am sure that if anyone ever asks my children what their mom's favorite saying was, they will calmly reply in unison, "How long do you want to live?"

I am a woman of low patience. My major concession to motherhood is the attempt to clean up my language. While I am sure it is equally true of other professions, the medical field is filled with rather prolific language. Most of our nonmedical terminology is of the three- and four-letter-word variety. I did not realize how graphic my language had become until I had children to mimic it for me. This usually occurs during inopportune moments, such as in church or when I am trying to impress someone.

When I started trying to eliminate profanity from my list of bad habits, I discovered it is a vice just like smoking or drinking. And like the addicted smoker who slips outside to sneak a puff, I find myself slipping out to the garage to enjoy a few muttered descriptive adjectives from time to time.

To compensate for the inability to let off steam with well-placed verbiage, I have settled for painting colorful word pictures. For instance, the phrase I heard most often as a child, "I'm gonna kick your butt over the moon!" has been changed to "I am going to launch your cute little derrière out of the solar system!" By using larger words, I find it is more difficult for them to repeat what I have said in polite company. Either it comes out so varied from the original that it is unrecognizable or it sounds so educated that people cannot believe it came from *my* kid!

In polling moms across the country, it became apparent that "Mom-isms" are universal and cross-generational. Some of the most-often-heard were:

1. "Because I *said* so!"
2. "I hope someday you have two children just like you."
3. "I know you can do better."
4. "Do I have to separate you two?"
5. "Wash behind your ears."
6. "Kill 'em with kindness."
7. "If your friends told you it was cool to jump off a bridge, would you follow them?"
8. "It's only because we love you."
9. "Just wait until your father comes home!"
10. "Why would a man buy a cow if he can get the milk for free?"
11. "I don't care *what* your friends do!"

12. "Pretty is as pretty does."
13. "Not now!"
14. "As long as you live in *my* house, you will follow *my* rules!"
15. "Children should be seen and not heard."
16. "No, honey, we can't afford it."
17. "You'll understand when you're older."
18. "If you tell the truth, you'll never have to remember what you said."
19. "What doesn't kill you will make you stronger."
20. "You'll always be my baby, no matter how old you grow."

Oh sure, I know there are a million other phrases you could think of, but this will get you started. It has been said that "when your children are little, they step on your toes, and when they are grown up, they step on your heart." While we try hard to impart all the pearls of wisdom we can to our children, we have to wonder at times whether they have understood one thing we tried to tell them. I guess it is true that you do understand when you are older, and it is only when those "Mom-isms" come out of your own mouth that your own mother can smile and know that you really were listening after all.

In the 1960s there was a lot of conversation about the "generation gap." We expounded endlessly over the vast difference between parents and children, a phenomenon contemplated throughout time and across generations. I don't know when it happened, but one day I woke up to find that I had fallen into the generation gap. One moment I was standing on the edge shaking my head and peering into the abyss, and the next minute I found myself standing at the bottom looking up and seeing someone shaking her head and looking down at me.

I think it all began when filling out one of those survey forms that ask for your age. For many years I had gaily and without thought checked the "18–34" box when volunteering my age. Then one day I found that I had migrated to the "35–54" box, and at that point "middle age" became not a colloquial term, but a reality.

Coincidentally, middle age invaded not only my mind, but my body. While I never considered myself particularly attractive, I consoled myself with the notion that I was at least thin, lithe, and reasonably intelligent. Now I find the answer is "D ... none of the above."

My husband told me recently I needn't worry about him having an affair because he is too fat. Obviously, his middle-aged self-talk has gotten to him, convincing him that his normal maturation process has left him unworthy of love. I think his comment is cause for great concern. After all, when is a person more vulnerable for an extramarital affair than when noticed and convinced that he "still has what it takes"?

I share his concerns over bodily changes caused by the ravages of time. I look in the mirror and see a face with impending wrinkles and graying hair staring back at me. I find unwanted hairs growing in strange localities around my body. I see a bloated belly untamed by sit-ups and dieting, a gut that leaves an eighteen-hour girdle quaking in its Spandex.

I see a waning energy level at a time of life when commitments keep me busy from dawn to dusk. Not that I want to question the power of God, but when I see Him face to face, I really want to know why He gives boundless energy to children who have no need of it and leaves none for the parents who must keep up with them.

I see a decreasing intellectual level. In the time it takes me to walk from the kitchen to the bedroom, I have often forgotten why I went there. All of my friends know if I don't enter an appointment in my Planner Pad, I probably will forget about it and not show up. When I lost this day-planner recently, I nearly had a panic attack, for all that I was, am, and ever hoped to be is logged in it. I ask you, is it stress or early Alzheimer's?

I fear for an uncertain future. The times, they are indeed "a-changin," and not necessarily for the better. I see my children growing up in a world without direction, with open hostility toward life. Even the "love songs" of today are filled with mistrust and frustration. Despite our efforts to provide our children with a head start, will it be enough? Will it *ever* be enough?

I look at my husband, standing before the bathroom mirror. He's staring at an ever-so-slightly wrinkled face, graying hair, a receding hair line (imperceptible to anyone but him). His center of gravity is dropping and taking his gut with it. He's still asking himself what he wants to be when he grows up, all the while realizing he may grow old without ever finding an answer. He worries about finances, college educations for his sons, retirement, and death, and whether he is a good father. I see a man who is lonely and broken and wondering if anything he has done has any meaning.

Standing there looking at him, I barely notice the paunch, the hair, the wrinkles. I see a man who is still the best-looking guy around. I see a man who would wreck the car to keep from hitting an animal. I see a man who does kind things and doesn't want any credit for it, a man who cries at sad movies. I see a man who has given his all to a job he never wanted, using his brilliant creativity to hold a family and a life together.

Sometimes I want to run to him and hold him, telling him how much I love him, and how proud I am of who he is and what he does. I want to thank him for providing a wonderful home for his family. I want to tell him he is just as sexy to me now as he was when I first met him, how I still want to spirit him off sometimes to savor him for myself.

I open my mouth to tell him, but the words won't come. Whether it is foolish pride or the twenty pounds of fat squashed by a Playtex girdle and stuffed into size ten slacks, I find myself breathlessly unable to tell him what is in my heart. My only hope is that while he watches me squeeze myself into an outfit that looked good ten years or twenty pounds ago, he'll see the good in me I often miss. I pray I'll learn to say the words before they don't matter anymore ... *I love you!*

Chapter 11
Anger and Other Maternal Instincts

I used to pride myself on my ability to find the humor in almost any situation. However, with the advent of children, I must admit that this ability is almost as nonexistent as my waistline.

I don't know how they do it, but my kids seem to have an innate ability to have me steaming like a hot tea kettle in an amazingly short time. My children are tied to me by invisible strings. With a mere blink of an eyebrow, they are able to pull those strings and control me with the skill of a seasoned puppeteer.

The trouble began when my children learned the word *no*. It is of no surprise to me that this was the first word out of their mouths … it was the one they heard most often. My question is, will they still remember it when they are teenagers?

Most recent psychology books advocate the sparing usage of the word *no*, saving it for extreme occasions. Obviously these psychologists do not live with my children. I find it difficult to imagine myself cheerfully encouraging my children to continue pulling the hair from the dog's tail. Neither can I see myself giving unerring approval to the creativity of the Picasso-like print adorning the wall, done completely in the last remnants of that fine makeup sold only in department stores.

I am incensed by the television commercial where two moms are chatting amicably, while in the background a kid yells, "*Mom, he spilled grape juice on the carpet!*" Had I been one of those two moms, some kid would have known the joy of space travel without the shuttle. But no! These two moms plaster inane grins on their faces and brainlessly reply, "That's okay." I can only guess that either both moms have the collective intelligence of a tsetse fly or were embroiled in a hot conversation and the grape juice situation did not completely register.

I recently attended a seminar on self-esteem, where the subject of anger was discussed. According to the speaker, when you are angry you are supposed to stop and ask yourself:

1. How mad should I be?
2. Is my anger fair?
3. How important will this event seem to me a year from now?

In most anger-producing situations I react, quickly and profusely. By the time I'd analyzed the above questions, I would probably forget what I was angry about in the first place ... and I guess that was the point.

Our seminar leader indicated we should imagine ourselves in a position of leadership and control. I envisioned myself as the pilot of an airplane. Then she instructed us to take control of our "self-talk," that being the things we say to ourselves. Instead of the blithering, blinding, furious words we usually say to ourselves when angry, she suggested we frequently repeat, "I am responsible. I am in control," while still envisioning ourselves in the position of leadership and control. She assured us that we are responsible for how we react to anger-producing situations.

I decided to put the theory into practice one day when my son chose to throw yet another of what had become his world-renowned temper tantrums. I took two deep breaths, then envisioned myself as the pilot of a huge airplane with many passengers on board. I was just becoming secure in the feeling that their lives were firmly and confidently in my control. As my son began whining about not wanting to go to school, I began my silent litany:

"I am responsible.

I am in control.

I am responsible.

I am in control."

As he launched into his tearful tirade regarding his inability to hang up his coat, the litany became faster.

"I am responsible.

I am in control.

I am responsible.

I am in control."

When my son began screaming, "*I hate school!* I want to go home!" I knew my pilot was in serious trouble.

"I *am* responsible!

I *am* in control!

I *am* responsible!

I *am* in control!"

When my son threw himself on the floor kicking and screaming, my pilot's fate was sealed.

"I *am* responsible!

I am *losing* control!

I am *not* responsible!

I am *not* in control!

Mayday!

Mayday!"

CRASH!

I erupted into my predictable fury, threatening to shorten my son's life span by about seventy years, all the while envisioning the burning rubble that was all that remained of my bold, beautiful pilot and her strong, powerful airplane. Yet another great theory had bitten the dust.

Have you ever found yourself jumping up and down screaming bloody murder at your kids, only to find them staring calmly back at you, drumming their fingers on the table in absolute boredom? That is when you have to ask yourself, "Who is the parent here?"

I am amazed at the flagrant disregard my kids seem to have toward my parental status. I couldn't wait to grow up and show my mom "how it was done," yet in reality it seems I seldom get up to bat. It seems my job has primarily boiled down to keeping the family ship from sinking. There is little time for an innovative thought or idea.

I don't think I got by with very much with my mom. Dad, by nature, was a pussycat. His favorite threat when really angry with me was to "kick my butt up between by shoulder blades," a threat on which he never followed through, I am thankful to report.

Mom, however, was 100 percent follow-through. No one could wield a Biff-N-Bat paddle like she could. I believe in all honesty that I was a stupid child. I constantly hounded my mom to buy Biff-N-Bat paddles. This is a wooden paddle with a red rubber ball connected by an elastic cord. It took no time at all to wear out the elastic cord, making it useless as a toy. On the other hand, the half-life of this paddle as a parental punishment device is infinitely longer. Why I continued to want them is still a mystery to me.

Mom could send you a withering look that would freeze misbehavior dead in its tracks. I have stood before the mirror for hours trying to recreate that look, but it never seems to work the same way for me.

Perhaps when it is all said and done, my children really do have my best interests at heart. Perhaps they know that if they were too good for too long, I would probably die of shock. At this rate, I'm guaranteed to be around for a good long time.

Chapter 12
Hormonal Hurricanes

There is a good reason why hurricanes are always given women's names. The adage "Hell hath no fury like a woman scorned" applies here. You will notice that a few tropical storms are given male names. That is because, while a man may fall into a depression, work up a good bluster, and rain all over you, only a woman can wither a branch with a look or level a house with raging hormonal fury. Doctors call it PMS; I call it a long-standing grudge from a higher deity.

Recall the biblical story about Adam, Eve, and the apple. For those of you unfamiliar with the story, it went something like this:

God created this beautiful world, perfect in every way. If He'd stopped there, things would have been great. But He took it an extra step and planted people in His creation, namely, Adam, the first man, and Eve, the first woman. This may have been His first faux pas. If God truly expected men and women to get along, I simply cannot understand why He made them so different.

Now, Adam was content to putter around the garden, pull some weeds, catch some rays, and occasionally holler, "Hey, Eve, what's for dinner?" Eve, being somewhat more complex, preferred shopping to domestic duty. One day while out scoping for bargains, she came across a huge tree, known by the natives as the Tree of Life.

Adam and Eve had both been warned not to eat the huge, red, ripe, sinfully delicious-looking apples on this tree. As she stood appreciating the perfect beauty of this truly organically grown marvel, a slimy serpent (precursor to the pushy salesperson of today) slithered up to her.

"Good afternoon," he said, sliding up behind her, nearly scaring her to death. "May I help you?"

"Oh, just looking," Eve nervously replied, embarrassed to have been caught in the Tree of Life Department.

"Aren't these apples stunning?" he said coyly, curling enticingly around the branch. "Best apples in the garden. Word is the Tree was flown in at great expense by the Big Kahuna Himself. And if you think these babies *look* great, just wait till you *taste* them!"

"Oh, I couldn't!" Eve cried, shocked yet vaguely intrigued at the prospect.

"Oh, but you could," the serpent replied, his voice oily with promise.

"But He told us specifically never to eat from this tree," she cried in protest.

"Best sales gimmick in the country," the serpent replied confidently. "Tell 'em they can't have it, and they will come in droves, dragging their VISA cards behind them. I tell you, little lady, one bite from one of these beautiful orbs, and you can have it all ... a happy family, a promising career, wealth beyond measure, and a husband who treats you as an equal, not just like someone made from a leftover rib."

Now that rib business had always stuck in Eve's craw. God had said she was created to stand *beside* Adam. Nowhere in the contract did it mention she could be relegated to cooking, keeping up the garden, and cleaning up after the animals while Adam sat on his duff.

"Besides," the serpent muttered demurely, "how can Adam complain? After all, apples have no fat and cholesterol, giving you that thin but voluptuous little body you've always craved. Best of all, though, it's absolutely *free!*"

Eve was a sucker for freebies. She bit, literally, and it hit the fan royally; the rest is history. The bottom line is that Eve got sold a bill of goods. As a result, thousands of years later women around the world are stuck with labor, menstrual cramps, and that "cross-this-line-and-you're-dead-meat!" feeling known as premenstrual syndrome, aka "hormonal hurricane."

Premenstrual syndrome is an amazing thing. One moment you are a sane, sensible adult, and then in the blink of an eye you are a blithering idiot, raging over some silly little thing like the kitten climbing up expensive curtains not yet paid for.

The key to survival from these hormonal outbursts is learning to relax. I have tried every form of relaxation therapy known to man. There was Transcendental Meditation, yoga, hypnosis, self-hypnosis, massage, acupressure, biofeedback, subliminal-message audio tapes, and exercise.

What I learned is that there are essentially three types of relaxation triggers: visual, auditory, and kinetic. Visual triggers are things that you can see, like a beautiful sunset or a beach. Auditory triggers are things you hear, like ocean waves or your favorite tunes on the radio. Kinetic triggers are things that can be touched, like a soft piece of velvet.

My very favorite method of relaxation combines visual and auditory triggers. I have long contended that there is nothing wrong with me that spending the rest of my life in an ocean-front condo couldn't take care of. Since the closest thing I have to an ocean is a drainage ditch known as Burnett's Creek, I bought an audio tape of ocean waves to listen to while driving in the car or before retiring for the night. The greatest hazard to an ocean tape is when you have to go to the bathroom while listening to it. The sound of all that water is a trigger for my bladder to empty itself, which can be a problem when driving in rush-hour traffic. It's even worse listening to the tape at night while sleeping in a waterbed! Still, ocean waves are always a hit with me, especially if I can also visualize myself on a Hawaiian island sipping a piña colada and reading a romantic novel …

Of all the things I ever tried, I found audio tapes to be the most satisfying. I did find the subliminal-memory improvement tapes seemed to help … when I remembered to listen to them. Probably the most amusing thing that happened on my quest for peace occurred during self-hypnosis. I had been faithfully listening to a relaxation tape in which the hypnotist asks the listener to take a deep breath and envision stepping onto an escalator going down. As you exhale, you are supposed to envision yourself going down, down, down … until total relaxation is obtained. Whenever I felt relaxed enough, I would stop and enjoy the quiet.

The trick to hypnosis tapes is in their repetition. The average person must hear a piece of information up to fifteen times before that knowledge becomes part of conscious thought. When relaxation tapes are used over consecutive days, the theory is, relaxation can be obtained more quickly and with less effort.

One day, while shopping at a local department store, I hopped on an escalator to a lower floor. As I began to go down, down, down the escalator, my eyes began to close, in trained response. I became so relaxed that at the bottom of the escalator I neglected to step off. I woke up abruptly to find myself sprawled face-first on the floor. It seems that in my oft-practiced self-hypnosis, I had never actually envisioned myself stepping off the escalator when the desired level of relaxation had been reached. We changed that practice real quick.

Everyone agrees that proper care of self includes stress management. "Take time for yourself!" we are told, but no one has yet been able to explain when exactly that is supposed to occur. If a woman elects to take on a hobby or relaxing activity that conflicts with family interests, she is labeled "selfish." My cat quilt and even the writing of this book have been relegated to late-night hours when I am "on call" rather than "on duty." How does one balance needs against desires?

They say that a woman's place is in the home … and in the grocery, and in the PTA, and in the workforce, and anywhere else that others don't want to go.

It seems the only time that people notice what a woman does is when she doesn't do it.

"How could you have forgotten to do that?" I am asked.

I contemplated the disparity between my husband's life and mine. As far as I can tell, the average morning for my husband goes something like this:

1. Get up … usually twenty minutes before work begins.
2. Shower.
3. Wash, dry, and style hair.
4. Brush teeth and shave.
5. Get dressed.
6. Kiss children good-bye.
7. Take out the trash every Friday.

My day is a bit more diverse. It goes something like this:

1. Get up … usually three hours before going in to work.
2. Dress and go walking for thirty minutes.
3. Get children up.
4. Shower and get re-dressed for work.
5. Set hair, do makeup, brush teeth.
6. Fix breakfast.
7. Do dishes.
8. Plan dinner.
9. Lay out vitamins and medicines.
10. Pick up dirty clothes and do laundry.
11. Straighten up the house.

12. Make beds.
13. Fix lunches.
14. Make sure four animals are fed.
15. Field phone calls and/or problems.
16. Fix "school snacks" monthly for each child.
17. Finalize car pool arrangements.
18. Referee fights.
19. Assure book bags are packed.
20. Assure chores are completed.
21. Help find shoes, coats, hats, and clothes not already packed.
22. Complete last-minute homework assignments.
23. Find last-minute homework assignments that mysteriously got lost two minutes before the bus was due to arrive.
24. Get the kids on the bus.
25. Deliver dog to babysitter's house (across the street from where the husband works).

Please note that most of my spouse's activities center around the care of himself. Most of my duties center around the care of everything *but* myself. While basic grooming is listed, it is often just a formality. Many days I have found myself getting in the car after a harrowing morning only to discover that my hair is still in rollers, and that I haven't a lick of makeup on. If I'm lucky, I am at least dressed!

Of course, for every ninety-nine women who will read these musings, smiling and nodding in perfect understanding and agreement, there will always be the one woman who says, "Oh, *my* husband is *nothing* like that!" He's the guy who cheerfully cooks, cleans the house, and takes care of the kids when his wife is unavailable. He would happily be the ultimate "house husband" if finances permitted. He encourages his wife to "go out with the girls," cheers on her every victory, and listens to the happenings in her day with rapt attention ... you know, your basic nightmare. My contention is that this woman is married to an alien, for I have known few male earthlings who fit into this pattern.

Then there is his female counterpart: "the little woman." She is the consummate cook, having tasty treats waiting for him whenever he wanders in and is hungry. She always looks perfect, never a hair out of place. She always defers to his good judgment and wouldn't think of putting him down. Sort of your Barbie and Ken arrangement. Unfortunately, this does describe what I thought marriage would be when Barbie and Ken were my role models for male–female relationships. However, when you consider Ken isn't even "anatomically correct," and Barbie has no cellulite and a waistline that any gnat would envy, I guess we should have realized that something wasn't quite right. Alas, even poor Barbie has caved in to the pressures of the future. The other day I heard two girls talking while playing with their Barbie dolls. Said one Barbie to the other, "Why don't I check my day planner, and we'll set a date to do lunch?" I guess her world has changed somewhat, too.

The basic "normal" marriage was the basis for the greeting card industry. Few things please me more than buying or receiving a great card. The more sarcastic or humorous, the better I like them. I have a couple of girlfriends who also enjoy buying and receiving these little missives. I can frequently be found giggling and guffawing in the Shoebox greeting card section of the local Hallmark store. In fact, I find this method of stress management infinitely cheaper than therapy. Since my best friend and I communicate mostly through rumor, these periodic humorous interludes are almost like having her in for a cup of coffee.

The other great treatment for "hormonal hurricane" is chocolate. Why Hershey hasn't created a chocolate pacifier for moms is beyond me; I think they'd make a killing! I can see it now—millions of women, driving the highways and byways of life, listening to ocean waves while sucking on a chocolate pacifier … gives new meaning to the phrase "life in the fast lane," doesn't it?

Chapter 13
Moving toward the American Dream

We moved around a lot when I was a child. In fact, I used to believe we moved more than an old woman on Ex-Lax. My father was always searching for something: a better job, more money, more satisfaction with his life. Today we call it reaching for that elusive American Dream. To a child, that dream seemed more like a nightmare.

Frequent relocations are both good and bad. The good side, although it also seems bad when it is happening, consists of constantly meeting new people, learning to adapt quickly to change, and seeing more of the country. I have met many people in my travels, some of whom I have managed to keep in my life all through the years.

The bad part about frequent moves is the total insecurity about oneself. It is like coming in on the middle of a half-told joke; the punch line rarely makes sense unless you know how the story started. The "new kid" always gets a lot of attention at first—usually in the form of close scrutiny. The newcomer spends a lot of time and effort trying to prove himself or herself worthy of befriending. Fortunately for me, someone always came to my rescue in that regard.

During my eighth grade year we moved twice, and the latter move was out of state. My initial feeling about the people of Michigan was that they were a cold and indifferent group who talked funny. For their part, they found an overly friendly girl who tried too hard and talked like a "hillbilly." My first attempts at friendship were met with cool stares and little else.

Then along came Wendy. Our first meeting came in physical education class. Back then everyone wore "gym suits," dull-colored, poorly fitting garments at best. But instead of being attired in the mandatory ugly red, she was truly outstanding in bright orange leotards and tights. Being a young lady of tall stature to begin with, I inwardly thought she resembled the Great Pumpkin.

"Who's that?" I asked, intrigued.

"Oh, that's the Great Pumpkin," they told me blandly. "She's weird—she thinks she's a vampire."

A vampire! That information was like waving a red flag in front of a bull and expecting it to stand still! It seemed that Wendy was indeed an eccentric who had few friends, and who spent an inordinate amount of time watching *Dark Shadows,* a daily soap opera that dealt with witches, vampires, and the like. However, for all her eccentricities, I soon found her to be the most intelligent girl I had ever met, whose high-minded principles were worthy of emulating.

Children can be so cruel, and especially so with strangers. Any deviation from the defined norm threatens to leave the newcomer alienated and alone. To find acceptance, new kids will often associate with whatever group accepts them first, often saying and doing things they might never have done if not seeking to find themselves.

To find themselves ... isn't that what everyone spends their lives doing? What is it we seek? What do we hope to find? What *is* the American Dream? For most of us it is the same elusive butterfly my father chased thirty years ago: job and financial security, close family relationships, and time to enjoy it all. What we are finding is also the same thing my father learned all those years ago. The reality is job insecurity, wages that cannot compete with rising prices, increasing cases of divorce, confused family values, and time commitments that leave no time to enjoy anything.

My father finally chose to relinquish the dream, deal with the nightmare, and get on with his life. He left the system, becoming unemployed for a time. He left his family and found a new one. I guess it was for the best, for he reports being happier and finally having the time to enjoy what he *does* have, which is his peace of mind.

That is the American Dream! It isn't new homes, or cars, or pools, or membership in the country club. It is looking in the mirror and liking who you see. It is knowing you have a friend and are a friend to others. It is picking up a hitchhiker without fearing for your life. It is kindness and love and caring … something the world has precious little of.

When our country was founded, the American Dream meant having a job to support the family. It meant having a place to raise your family. It meant having the opportunity to prove your abilities. The belief was that if one was willing to work hard, all things were possible.

Where are the jobs? They're in Mexico, South America, China, and Japan. We need to return them to the United States. And once they are returned, we need to take better care of them. Who we are is largely tied to what we do. When we're unemployed a large chunk of who we are disappears with the job.

Do we *need* large, expensive houses, or would a paid-for smaller home do just as well? Do our kids *need* expensive vacations and participation in every extracurricular event, or would they prefer a family baseball game in the backyard or a picnic in the park? Would they perhaps rather have our *time?*

Perhaps we need to reevaluate the American Dream. It seems that after two hundred–plus years, we still seek the same goals we came here for and yet are seemingly further away than ever before.

The dream is tarnished by get–rich schemes, lotteries, and megadollar magazine giveaways. I will admit I'm the first to get my entries in to Publishers Clearing House, dreaming of the day when the Prize Patrol visits my house. It will probably happen on the day when every toy is scattered across the living room floor, as the dust bunnies are skittering across the linoleum. I'll no doubt answer the door looking like the poster child for "Can This Face Be Saved?"

I must also admit to standing in a ridiculously long line to obtain a lottery ticket the day the Powerball hit 110 million dollars. I find it obscene that one person won the whole pot; obscene only in how much better it would have been for more than one person to know a little security.

Just imagine—$100 given to one million people would make them somewhat happier. One thousand dollars given to 100,000 people would make them much happier. Ten thousand people given $10,000 would have cause for ecstasy. One hundred thousand dollars would cure most of the financial ills of a thousand people. And a hundred people given a million dollars would be considered filthy rich in most segments of society.

Happy people spend money. Increased spending creates jobs. More jobs mean more people have money to spend. That delicate balance must be maintained if we are to continue to grow and prosper.

Maybe the whole trick is in being happy with what you have and saving for the future. I think I'll start by saving the postage I have sent in to Publishers Clearing House for the last ten years. As often as I receive their flyers, I could be in Tahïti for a luxury vacation in five years!

THE FAMILY CIRCUS® By Bil Keane

"Yesterday's the past, tomorrow's
the future, but today is a GIFT.
That's why it's called
the present."

Chapter 14
The Sower of Seeds

I had hoped to keep this book a rather lighthearted piece on the joys and frustrations of motherhood. But, as so often happens, recent events have brought a new perspective to the concepts of love and family. Sometimes being a mom just isn't very funny.

I have spent a number of years working as a nurse in an emergency care setting. In that time I have seen many joys and sorrows of the human experience. For seven years I also served as an Emergency First Responder for my rural community, a volunteer job that also brought both pride and frustration. Because we were a small unit, we were constantly on call, responding whenever we were home. During those years, I never knew the joy of sitting around in robe and slippers, totally relaxed. My kids grew up knowing that when the pager went off, they were to get to the car immediately. There was always a sense of the unexpected, something lurking around the corner.

A call for help came one afternoon while we were sitting around the pool with friends—a possible drowning, no other information. Upon arriving at the scene we found a four-year-old child, with resuscitation efforts already in progress. To a medical professional such sights are tragic but common. It is easy to become concerned about heart rhythms, doing CPR, placing tubes and intravenous lines, and waiting for a response. What is not easy is realizing there is a four-year-old child lying under all the apparatus whose life hangs in the balance. Still, if emergency service personnel stop to think about that, it becomes too overwhelming to do the job. One must dissociate to protect oneself from the tragedies of life.

As the child was loaded onto the ambulance with full resuscitation ongoing, we noticed the yard was littered with leftover packages, needles and unused equipment left behind. Feeling fearful that the child might not survive, we returned to pick up and straighten the area so that the parents would not have to see it upon their return.

It was then that I saw her ... the mother of the child, so beautiful, so frightened, so alone. Knowing she should not drive to the hospital on her own, I volunteered to drive her there. Without realizing it, I had emotionally switched gears. Once in the car, she asked me whether her child would live. I immediately launched into every nursing platitude I had ever known about the resilience of children, the improved chances of a cold-water drowning, the fact that her child had been found quickly and resuscitation begun. But the platitudes rang hollow and empty; in our hearts we both feared the child would die.

Without conscious thought, I went from a seasoned (and, *I thought,* well-insulated) professional to the level of fellow-woman, fellow-mom, fellow-caring person. As we flew down the country back roads that sunny warm day, I felt as though I had become a surrogate (if temporary) family member. I heard the mother's self-recriminations. We cried and prayed all the way to the hospital. She had quit her job to be home with her son because she had worried so about him when she worked, about whether he was happy. She told me about the wonder of his smiles, hugs, and laughter. She told me how happy they had been together that day. She said that only a few days before, the child had asked whether when you went to heaven you could eat anything you wanted.

By the time we reached the hospital, little Justin had become a part of my life. We walked toward the emergency room entrance, both weak-kneed and fearing the news ahead. When the bad news came, we cried and held each other, sharing our grief. She cried for her child; I cried for her.

As she held the blue and lifeless form of what had moments before been a beautiful, brown-eyed, fair-haired child, we wept. As I looked into the glazed and empty eyes of the child that had been, I saw the face of my own four-year-old, brown-eyed, fair-haired child. I had left him at the pool in the care of my friend, and now all I wanted to do was run home as quickly as possible and hold him to me.

She wanted to hold her child, to rock him one last time. She held her little boy, bundled in a blanket with all the tubes in place, and wept. She apologized to him for letting him down. She told him that yes, in heaven you can eat whatever you want, whenever you want. She told him how precious he had been to her life.

As I struggled to regain control of my emotions, I paused to see how my fellow professionals were handling things and made an important discovery ... their shields were up. They had concerned themselves with heart rhythms, CPR, placing tubes and intravenous lines, and waiting for a response. While they realized a four-year-old boy lay under the apparatus, he wasn't real to them yet. This is not to say that the medical professionals were cold and uncaring. When the code is called, and family is allowed within the inner sanctum of the shock room, the victim becomes real. We hear the screams of shock, see the bitter tears, provide hugs and hot coffee, and make appropriate calls to family and funeral homes.

Once the family arrives, we return to our own units to admit the defeat of death. Often we retreat to bathrooms to shed tears for the families left behind. We may spend a few sleepless nights crying for the patient who couldn't be saved. We rail at a faceless God for the seeming unfairness of life. Up in the intensive care unit, there is probably an old and frail body, racked with pain, clinging to life while praying for death, while elsewhere a young child's life is abruptly snatched away. The search for understanding is fruitless. The pain becomes a dull ache that leaves within a few days or weeks. We don't generally keep contact with the family, and the loss is not our own.

The loss is not our own. Then *why* did I feel such grief? This pain was searing and knifelike, the hole torn as gaping as the one that sank the *Titanic*. I felt I had no right to feel so bad. I had lost *nothing!* Then I began to see the faces of the relatives and friends I had lost to death. The names and faces of patients I had cared for flashed before my eyes, and I cried for them, one and all. Over the next weeks, I flushed out more tears and recalled more pain than I even knew I could feel. The realization finally came that I had stored up fifteen years of pain. I had held my grief at arm's length and never let it in. Now it was in, and I thought I would surely die from it.

I replayed in my mind every word that grieving woman had said and applied it to my own life. She blamed herself for the accident. Justin had been playing in the sandbox near the house when she went inside to use the bathroom and get a drink of water. She didn't tell him not to go near the pond—she had never needed to. He had always been afraid of the water. She trusted him.

Every mother learns to trust her child. It is an important process in building autonomy for both mother and child. It has been said that mothers and children spend a lifetime trying to break free from each other. In a child's infancy and the toddler stage, the mother must be constantly watchful, for young children have little concept of danger. As children grow, so does a mother's trust. We trust them to dress themselves, then play outside alone, to ride their bikes in the street, to go to the homes of friends, to date, to drive our cars, and finally to move out and begin lives of their own. It is a long path, filled with laughter and tears. For this mother the path was cut short.

She had given up her job out of concern for her son's safety and happiness. In doing so, she had given him the greatest gift any mom can give—her time and attention. While I had paid lip service to the importance of my children, they had been just another aspect of my life. They were often pulled here and there at the whim of my job. They had been jerked out of bed at ungodly hours to get to the sitter's house. While they were fortunate to have good sitters, they always preferred days at home, to sleep in their own beds and play with their own toys. The cold facts were that I had not built a world for them, but rather had dragged them through mine.

This mother had told me about conversations held with her child that day. In looking at my own life, I saw that I'd been so busy filling my "day off" with cooking, cleaning, doing laundry, and paying bills that I couldn't remember having a single conversation with my children that didn't being with "Don't!" or "Stop that!"

For the next week, I didn't raise my voice to the kids one time. I realized that a lot of my anger had disappeared. I have spent years wondering why I am such an angry person. I have paid counselors a fortune to try to unravel the confused threads of my life.

People always seek a reason for the death of a loved one, but never more than when a child dies. For those with a belief in a higher deity and a hereafter, there is some comfort. Imagine how empty death must seem to one who does not have this belief! It took the death of an innocent four-year-old boy to help me see that the invisible shield I had put up to protect me from pain at work was also up at home. It was up to protect me from a less-than-perfect marriage, from the pain of my parents' broken marriage. It was up to protect me from the knowledge of my own failure as a wife and parent.

For me, Justin's death was a catalyst for change. While he was snatched from his mother's arms in a second, I was losing my children in inches. Through overcommitment, an unstable marriage, and a dual-career situation, I just didn't "have time" for my family!

For weeks I was up late at night, watching my sons breathe, grateful for each breath they took. During the days I began to watch them, *really* watch them, to share in their joys and triumphs. I took more time to play and actively listen. I had let them in, and I was learning to love them as unconditionally as I knew how.

The changes came gradually. First to go were the extra hours at work, and next the First Response Team; finally, we entered into family counseling. While I don't expect perfect healing in this lifetime, I will remain eternally grateful to Justin for showing me a need and to God for showing me the way.

I would later hear that a beautiful daughter was born to Justin's parents. Despite the tragedy that had come before, life had come full circle for these two very deserving parents. While this precious child will never replace Justin in their hearts and minds, she is the promise that life does indeed go on and, like the circle, has neither a distinct beginning nor a definitive end. Perhaps we can *all* find comfort in that!

The Sower Of Seeds

One day the Father looked around
All Heaven 'til he found
A fair-haired boy with eyes of brown
Planting seeds upon the ground.

"My child," He said with radiant smile
"I know you like it here,
But I've a woman down on Earth
Who needs a dose of cheer.

"I don't know just how long you'll stay,
But give her lots of love,
And somehow always let her know
Her gift came from above."

"Yes, Sir!" the little lad replied,
And down to Earth he came.
One bright March morn, the child was born,
And Justin was his name.

He was her joy, her life, her all.
She watched him as he grew,
And she was always so surprised
At all the things he knew.

At four years old he was so bright
To a hundred he could count.
As she watched him playing T-ball
Her love knew no amount.

77

Jan Blackburn

None knew he was an angel
For his wings had never shown;
His job was just to smile and play
While seeds of love were sown.

One day his work on Earth was done,
And he was called back home.
Her heart was filled with empty tears.
She felt so all alone.

Each day and night she railed at God.
Through angry tears she prayed,
"How could You give this precious gift,
And then take it away?"

"My lovely child," the Father said.
"I know you feel such pain.
I know right now you feel you'll never
Smile and laugh again.

"But look inside and see the gift
That Justin left for you.
He left you seeds of love and hope,
Of life begun anew.

"When given the light of laughter
And watered by your tears
Small seeds of hope will sprout within
To hold throughout the years.

"Justin taught you how to love,
Put his needs before your own.
In leaving it was not his wish
To leave you all alone.

"The seedlings you may choose to pluck
And fling them far from you,
But better still to do with them
What he would have you do.

"Share those tiny sprouts of hope
With others who have none.
Find completion of the job
That Justin had begun.

"Give meaning to the precious life
You held but for a while.
Remembering the quiet hugs
His gentle loving smile.

"Don't mourn the child that you have lost
For he is safe with me.
He waits to share all he has learned
Throughout eternity."

—For Justin
7/20/1993

Chapter 15
Dorothy—The Eulogy
I Never Gave

When I was twenty-eight years old, my father left home, and my parents subsequently divorced. Of one hundred people polled, I was probably the only one who was surprised by this announcement. I realized their marriage was not a perfect one by any stretch of the imagination, but somehow I always believed that their faith in God and brute determination would carry them through. My father had been working a construction job in southern Indiana and had sought temporary housing with an older woman who was widowed and taking in boarders to help pay the bills. When he moved out of our home, he moved in with Dorothy in what would become a permanent move. I don't believe I ever blamed Dorothy for this; the only blame I could ascribe to her was that she had made it easier for my father to make his ultimate move.

I guess one of my many faults is that I need to label people, so I know how they fit into my world. Dorothy floated around for years without a label. When asked about her, my father was rather vague, saying first that Dorothy was his landlord, and later his friend. Even when he announced her as his wife, she had no place in my life. He never said he loved her; he laughingly said they had married so that everyone would quit talking about them.

I spent a lot of time being angry with my father for leaving. It was easy to blame his defection on a midlife crisis, for I saw both of my parents seemingly turn their backs on most of the values they had worked so hard to instill in me. My dad had always been a quiet, clean-cut guy, who dressed conservatively and went to church every Sunday.

One weekend several months after he had left, he made the three-hour journey to visit my home. When I opened the door to greet him, I saw a fifty-year-old guy with *long* hair and a scraggly beard and mustache! He wore faded jeans with a cowboy hat and boots. He wore a plain white undershirt and had developed a paunch. He wasn't the man I had defined as father.

While it was good to see him, it was nonetheless awkward. We didn't have much to say to each other. He wanted to share his new hobby, playing the fiddle. When he left I felt *very* empty and sad. I felt like the father I had known had died. It was the last time my father would come alone.

Henceforth, Dad would bring Dorothy when he came to visit. Dorothy was an unusual woman, with five or six grown children and multiple grandchildren. They were a tight-knit family who enjoyed being together and seemed to accept my father as one of the group. When I visited I felt like I was totally out of my league. As an only child, I was jealous at sharing my Dad's attention with my older "step-siblings."

I could never seem to get my Dad off by himself, and even when I could, our conversations were closed and stilted. It became easier not to even try. In fact, it became increasingly easier to believe that I didn't need *any* of them. I built high emotional barriers to protect myself from hurting.

Dorothy and I would develop an uneasy truce, and eventually I got used to her ways and she to mine. I still couldn't see exactly what my father saw in her, and he remained unable to tell me. I would see him do little things for her that he would never have done for my mom. In a way that irked me, for I felt that if he would have done some of those things for my mom, perhaps things might have been different. Yet I realized he must care for her or he wouldn't be doing all those things.

On December 23, 1994, Dorothy had a serious heart attack. She went into cardiac arrest shortly after her arrival to the hospital. The doctors said her only hope for survival was to undergo bypass surgery.

The night before her surgery I spoke with her, and she asked me to come down to be with my dad. On the drive to Louisville, Kentucky, I had a lot of time to think … and to worry. It suddenly occurred to me that her family would be there, too. I grew anxious, worrying about how they would respond to my presence. I had met only one or two of them, and that was long before Dad and Dorothy had married. Were they as confused about the relationship as I was?

When I entered the waiting room, my Dad had stepped out. I recognized Dorothy's son Donald, who rose and greeted me warmly. Then he turned and introduced me to the others.

"This is your sister, Jan," he said. They all greeted me equally warmly. I couldn't have asked for a better reception. They invited me into their family seemingly without hesitation. I learned then that I had five step-brothers, one step-sister, forty-nine step-nieces and nephews, and their children. Suddenly I had gone from being the only child of an only child to having a *huge* family!

I listened to Dorothy's family reminisce about her. I heard stories about her warmth and caring and love for her family. I began to see her in a whole new way. Later, at the hotel and over dinner, my Dad and I began to talk. We stayed up until three o'clock in the morning and talked for over six hours. We said all of the things we had needed to say for over twelve years!

He told me that Dorothy was his best friend. He told me how lonely he had been. He said Dorothy never put him down, only encouraged him. He told me how people laughed at her sometimes and how a little child had told her one time that she was ugly, and how hurt she had been.

Dad told me how lost he would be if she didn't survive the surgery. I found myself envying how much he cared about her—not just her having that much of his attention but having someone who loves you *that* much. I began to see her as someone special. I regretted all the time I had lost due to ignorance and pride. I hadn't allowed my father the right to feel lonely or the need to be truly loved, and I almost lost him because of it. I hadn't seen the strength and inner beauty of Dorothy, and because of that I had missed the opportunity to see the woman my Dad saw. I had very nearly missed the opportunity to maybe have a new family, with all the adventures that go with it. Most of all, I had wasted twelve long years being angry for essentially *nothing!* I learned then that not everything is as we *see* it.

Dorothy had a serious stroke three days after surgery. Severely weakened, she needed a ventilator to help her breathe. Her speech had been affected. At one time I had wished she didn't talk so much; now I only wished I could have a conversation with her. I wanted to apologize for being such a fool. I wanted the chance to begin again. Life is so very short; I thought I had learned that. I shall always regret the angry words spoken between my grandmother and me the night before she died. None of us know whether we will have tomorrow to apologize for our folly.

A marriage proverb in the Bible tells us we should "never let the sun go down on our anger." So it should be with all the important people in our lives. Wealth and fame are short-lived and often fade with time; only friendship and love will stand the test of time.

At 2:30 in the morning on January 29, 1995, Dorothy passed on into eternity. She has shed the outward shell she wore on earth and wears the perfection of her inner beauty. Her kindness and caring is now all we see of Dorothy. It lives on in the hearts and minds of all who truly knew and loved her.

It has been said that you are dead only when you are forgotten. If that is true, then Dorothy will live on for a good long time. I know my father will remember her kindness every day of his life. He described her as his "best friend in life" and was convinced he would never find another woman like her.

I cannot grieve for Dorothy, for I believe she is in a far better place. Had she lived, she would have been permanently paralyzed and would probably have never talked clearly, something she would never have condoned. She fought hard for her life, her family, and her husband but was foiled by the frailties of the flesh.

I grieved for my dad. Dorothy had lifted him from the depths of despair and given him that thing he had spent his whole life looking for … himself. Though much of their time together was spent in financial instability, they told that to no one, keeping their pride and dignity intact. She encouraged him to relax more, to take time for himself, and encouraged his fiddle playing. She went everywhere with him and learned to like his music. During the week after the funeral, I really listened to my dad play his fiddle, and I have to admit that he has gotten pretty good. My dad told me how self-conscious Dorothy was about her looks, saying at first she hadn't wanted to leave the house. He said that people often laughed at her behind her back, especially after her first stroke. Dad began wearing bib overalls, saying, "If they're going to laugh at you, they might as well laugh at me, too." That seemed to appeal to her sense of justice, and she also began to relax. They were good for each other.

I grieve for Dorothy's children. Dorothy complained bitterly about how infrequently she saw or talked to her family, even though she saw them often by most people's standards today. I frequently found myself defending them, knowing how rapidly my days, weeks, and months go flying by. I rarely saw Dad and Dorothy myself, somehow always believing I would take the time tomorrow, or next week, or next month.

But now the time is gone. I didn't get to tell her I am sorry and how wrong I was. I grieve for myself and the relationship I could have had with Dorothy. I grieve for the family I *could* have had. I grieve for the years I spent in anger or indifference. It would seem that I learn my best life lessons retrospectively.

Dorothy taught lessons to all of her family and friends by her example. Much of what I know of Dorothy I learned from my father and unfortunately it came at the end of her life. I cannot correct the mistakes I made with her, but I can learn from what she taught, both by her life and her death. The lessons I learned are as follows:

1. Don't judge a book by its cover. By concentrating on the outer shell I nearly missed the beautiful pearl within.
2. Call your mother (or father). Dorothy's day could be made or broken by whether she heard from one of her family members on any given day. While now I often long for the peace and quiet afforded by the absence of my children, I suspect I will indeed miss them when they are gone and will long to listen to their voices and the stories of their lives.
3. Take time. Today could be the last chance that any of us has to lend an ear, confess or profess our love, share a bit of ourselves, or learn from someone else.

Time would eventually ease my father's grief, and in November 1995 he married for the third time, to my stepmother Edna. I have tried not to make the same mistakes with this new lady in my life, and I can tell you that it has been a happy relationship right from the start. They show me every day by their example how good a marriage can be. I love being the eldest daughter of this new family, so now, without even trying, I have gone from being an only child, to the youngest of the second, and to the oldest of the third family. Therefore, I can tell you that I have every neurosis that comes with each birth ranking! I've learned about sharing, caring, and how great it is to have someone to share a parent with.

I wonder sometimes how Dorothy's children feel about his remarriage. I wonder whether they feel he has forgotten his best friend. I want them to know that I believe Dorothy will in some way remain with my father always.

Dorothy's journey through life is complete. I firmly believe she has been reunited with her beloved first husband, Oscar. Dad's journey is not yet completed, and there are many twists and turns left to his journey.

I will never be able to thank Dorothy in this life for the precious gift she gave my dad, but I want her family to know that I know that thanks needs to be given. I have always believed that people are brought into our lives for a reason. It is also my belief that Dorothy's purpose in my dad's life was to restore peace and harmony to his soul. The rest is like a new diary, with blank pages just ready and waiting to be filled with adventures, joys, sorrows, and all the other little things that keep life so very entertaining!

When the Casseroles Stop Coming

When the casseroles stop coming,
Cards of consolation tossed,
I hope someone will still recall
That I am feeling lost.

While others will have gone
Back to their work and to their play,
For me time will have frozen when
My loved one passed away.

I'll need to talk about my loss
Next day, next month, next year,
For memories are all I have
Of one I loved so dear.

So be the kind and loving friend
You've now and always been,
And listen to my oft-told tales
And memories once again.

One day I shall repay this debt
When you are feeling blue,
And when the casseroles stop coming,
I'll be right there for you.

7/15/1993

Chapter 16
Remodeling Is a Four-Letter Word

Remodeling is a four-letter word. I should know, since I have said most of them during our most recent attempt at home improvement. My husband and I have a penchant for taking a lost cause and making it lose even more. When we first married, we bought a small house and completely remodeled it. When we started having children, it became apparent that two bedrooms and one bathroom wouldn't suffice. Additionally, we had no yard and lived entirely too close to a busy highway.

Finding available property in our small town is a rarity, but we finally found a nice little place, well off the highway and on an acre of ground. It also had just two bedrooms and one bathroom, but with all the yard space, we were unconcerned about having room to add on. That was our first mistake.

Our first hurdle was in deciding on a floor plan. Since my husband is artistically inclined, he has designed most of the many remodeling projects we have done together. He spent many nights drawing and redrawing. No matter how we planned it, there would be a tree, a septic tank, a leach bed, something that would inevitably hamper our plans. Finally, we decided on a plan and began what would become years of sawing, banging, buying, doing, and redoing—the hallmarks of remodeling.

My children grew up with the same construction crew, first in one house and then the other. The kids were so accustomed to seeing them that one day when they entered the house to start the day's work, my youngest son hollered, "Hey, Mom, Pete's home!"

To their credit I must say that our builders have done a great job in this remodeling project. It truly is a nice job, and we can't be the easiest people to work for. Every time they got one project completed, we decided we should have done it differently, and so we began over again. I also have a perfectionist "artist type" for a husband. He can see it, draw it, and then expect the builders to reproduce it. Sometimes that has not been humanly possible.

I did pretty well for the first three years, but this last six months has really gotten me down. I'm beginning to think we were not destined to complete this project. We were within three to four weeks of completion when Murphy's Law went into effect … everything that *could* go wrong *did* go wrong.

It all started in the stairwell. The first paint job in the stairwell was nearly perfect. During the staining of the stair treads, a little stain got on the wall, so it was repainted. Somehow a diagonal strip ended up on the wall. After a couple of attempts to repaint, the wall was sanded and sprayed. Some of the newly installed woodwork got sprayed also.

Meanwhile, the cabinet tops for the bathrooms were back-ordered several weeks. Everything came to a screeching halt while we waited for the backsplashes. When they finally arrived, the colors were reversed. When the colors were corrected, the backsplashes no longer fit on the countertop. In the downstairs bathroom the plumber elected to cut a large hole in the vanity rather than moving the plumbing pipe where it should have been, leaving a gaping hole in the back of the vanity.

We were delighted when the soft pleated shade was hung in the bedroom, relatively without incident. Three weeks later we discovered that Mildred, the aforementioned "dog from hell," had chewed off the cord, leaving us unable to lower the blind.

Feeling stressed to capacity, we elected to take a brief vacation, hoping against hope that things would be better when we returned. … Wrong. We just took our bad luck with us. The video camera went out about ten minutes into the long-awaited Disney World vacation with the kids. The 35mm camera went down the second day.

Home once more, we found our streak of bad luck had only begun. The above-ground pool had sprung a leak, thanks to some rather enterprising moles that had burrowed under the liner. I can only hope that when the seam ripped and water flooded into their homes, they had some idea of how mad I was! A new liner was required, and a one-way ticket was procured for the moles. Now, if you have ever had a mole problem, you know that everyone has a possible cure for these little vagrants. But as one of my patients so aptly put it, "It really doesn't do any good to kill one mole, because six more come to the funeral."

One of the things I hate most about vacations is the mountain of laundry that must be done upon returning home. After doing ten loads of laundry, we discovered that the washer and dryer had also broken down.

Next on the break-down train was the riding lawn mower. After mowing the grass with a push-mower and raking that wonderful acre of yard once or twice, we promptly went out and invested in a new riding lawn mower and grass sweeper.

All of the above happened in a three-week period. We began to dread waking up in the morning, wondering what else would break down, fall apart, or need repair. The house had been a trash pit for months. At first I tried to stay ahead of the dirt, dust, and mess, but finally I fell into despair and went on strike. I decided I would just wait and clean the whole thing up at one time. By the time I realized move-in day would take months instead of days or weeks, the dust bunnies had staked a claim on the house. We couldn't breathe in the bedroom without choking on dust. When my husband got under the bed to unplug the light bar before leaving on vacation, he almost couldn't find it!

We finally have elected to relax and realize that this project is not the most important thing in our lives. With that decision made, life is getting much better. I have decided, however, that if we ever do finish this project, I never want to hear the words *change* or *remodel* ever again. I prefer to think of this in the same way I do pregnancy … worth the effort but something I never want to do again!

Chapter 17
It's a Woman Thing

I don't know if it is genetic or a trained response, but women often feel that they are taken for granted. I have been advised that men also feel this way but usually not on a daily basis. Most of the women that I know feel they cannot make major policy decisions in the house without a man's guidance. Even minor repair jobs seem to go easier with a man's influence. Women who have never married and those who are really sure of themselves may not agree with this statement, but it sure is true for me.

Even my next-door neighbor occasionally feels the pinch. She has been divorced for several years and seems pretty sure of herself; but when she went car shopping, she informed the salesman she would not buy until she brought a man with her to check the deal. Without a doubt, women are often sold a bill of goods when it comes to repairs and purchases, by men who apparently think women don't have the good sense to ask the proper questions. Maybe that goes back all the way to Eve, but when women "take the bite" and enter into a man's domain, they often suffer the consequences.

I am definitely a sucker for a sales pitch. My husband is constantly amazed by how absolutely naive I can be. One day the *World Book Encyclopedia* representative came to my door. His pitch was so convincing that I found myself believing that I would be a neglectful parent if I didn't have these wonderful books available when my child was ready and that my child would be bypassed in the world of opportunities because he was not *World Book*-literate.

When my husband came home, I was waist-deep in encyclopedias, *Young Scientist*, easy reading books, and a primary encyclopedia set. I was just about to sign on the dotted line when my husband asked if we could speak privately.

"What exactly are you doing?" he asked reasonably.

"I'm securing my child's future," I calmly assured him. "When he is ready, I will lay the world of information at his feet."

"He's two years old! By the time he is old enough to read, the world will have changed and these books will be obsolete!" He stormed out, completely disgusted with my complete lack of sales resistance. I was left with the unsavory job of politely tossing this poor salesman gently out on his ear, and he no doubt departed wishing that my husband had been left in traffic with a flat tire.

I seem to go through crazies where I am completely enchanted with a product or belief process. Whether it is cookware, makeup, or vitamins, it is "out with the old and in with the new." My family usually groans, wondering what new device I have for torturing them now. Their philosophy seems to be "sigh and comply," knowing that like a tropical storm, my blustering winds of high excitement will eventually die down and we will return to normal. They just take that for granted.

Unfortunately, I also feel taken for granted. It has somehow been assumed that there will always be clean clothes, a clean house, groceries in the fridge, and bills paid, with no sweat on their part. I know that this is true, because the other day I overheard my son tell a friend that they didn't need to clean up their mess: "My Mom will take care of it." I bet he doesn't make *that* mistake again!

Now I didn't use to mind the inconsideration all that much, because there were fringe benefits, like living in a comfortable house and having two incomes to pay the bills, and of course, there were always birthdays, anniversaries, Mother's Day, and Christmas holidays where my family could show their appreciation. However, in recent years I find not only that our anniversary passes by unnoticed, but that I barely remember having a birthday, and that last Mother's Day went by without a card! At least Christmas is still intact.

Meanwhile, I work with a girl whose every whim seems to be indulged. All holidays are marked with gifts, with diamonds occurring every five years of their marriage. I found myself wanting to flush her head down the toilet when she came in sporting diamond earrings for their fifteen-year anniversary. Now, I realize that it isn't gifts and presents that make a family, but these treasures sure don't *hurt* anything!

I also feel taken for granted at work. Every employer seems to feel that the job should come first in a person's life. For many years I think it did, taking precedence over family and friends. The other day I was asked to come in during my vacation to attend a meeting. I politely declined.

"But it's your day off!" I was told.

"I don't have days off," I replied. "On the days I don't work for you, I am working as an au pair girl for a family—a man and his two sons. I cook for them, clean for them, and generally take care of them."

"Oh, you poor dear!" she sympathized. "All that in addition to caring for your *own* family!"

"They *are* my own family!" I replied as I walked away.

Chapter 18
If Every Day Were Mother's Day

One bright and sunny May morning, I was awakened by the sounds of whispering voices. Smiling to myself, I realized that a Mother's Day conference was occurring. Soon I was presented with a menu of breakfast choices in a childish scrawl:

> *Meneu*
>
> *Brecfest, ornge juece*
> *cold cerel coffee*
> *hot ", begal, taster strootle.*

After I made my selections, my eight-year-old waiter advised me that we were out of orange juice and bagels, and that he didn't know how to make coffee or hot cereal, but he *could* make me a bowl of Special K. It didn't matter; what truly mattered was that he *wanted* to do something thoughtful. It was on that day that I taught my sons how to make refrigerator cinnamon rolls and coffee, a staple in the single man's diet. I smiled to myself as he began to relate to me what my "choices" for lunch and supper would be.

My son was even thoughtful enough to plan my day's activities for me. First I was advised that my sons would vacate the house so I could read or relax. Then it was concluded that since they would need to have someone accompany them to the park, perhaps I would prefer to join them in roller-blading or playing baseball. I have to admit that playing second base was much more fun than curling up with a great book in a quiet house.

I used to think that Mother's Day was just another reason for the greeting card companies to create another pseudo holiday. I must admit that since I have become a mother, I actually enjoy this particular "holiday." It isn't just the presents that I enjoy; it's the creativity that goes into them. One year I got a coupon book good for free cleaning and other chores around the house. Mostly it is just feeling special for a day. If I could ask for anything, however, it would be to experience this feeling more than just once a year. That is what I believe everyone wants ... just to feel special and that perhaps we belong to something important.

In the 1970s we began to hear about the "women's movement." It started out about equal pay for equal jobs. It quickly migrated into issues regarding abortion rights, sexual discrimination, and sexual harassment, and the list goes on. We have asked, begged, and pleaded for men to come to our way of thinking, essentially to become more like us. Now that we have pretty well succeeded in emasculating them, we complain bitterly that "you just can't find a *real* man anymore!" No wonder men are confused ... I'm not sure that I understand it myself!

Our children are growing up learning about human rights, but I find myself wondering just who is writing the instruction manual. We preach "just say no" to drugs and alcohol, but both seemingly are becoming easier for mere children to obtain. We teach them about the nightmare of AIDS, telling our children that the best way to avoid it is sexual abstention. Then, out of the other side of our mouths, we also preach "safe sex"—at least use a condom. Instead of assuring that our children can read, write, and do arithmetic, they spend precious hours learning how to apply a condom and become a "socially correct" individual.

We tell our children to accept alternative lifestyles, telling them that it is perfectly all right to be asexual, bisexual, homosexual—just *be yourself*—whoever that is! We push and drive our children to be the best and brightest, often pushing them to grow up way before they are ready, and then wonder why teenage pregnancy, criminal behavior, and substance abuse are ballooning out of control. I think if I were a child in today's society, I would try to escape, too!

When I was an adolescent, the philosophy was "don't trust anyone over thirty." Today's children are growing up learning "don't trust anyone—period." Our generation grew up fearing we would be annihilated by a nuclear holocaust. Today's kids have a greater fear of being killed by gang violence or a drive-by shooting. In retrospect I think I grew up in a fairly sheltered environment. As a parent I find myself unable to spread myself thin enough to shield them from everything that will be coming at them from all directions. I have often laughed that my sons' guardian angels had better be taking their coffee breaks now, because when those two hit adolescence they may never get a good night's sleep again ... I know *I* won't!

I recently stood beside my sister-in-law as we said good-bye to my eldest niece. She left our sleepy-eyed village to venture off to an out-of-state college. We shed tears at her departure, not even sure of what we were crying about. I know we will miss her, but maybe a part of us is a little envious at the potential that lies ahead for her. Maybe some of our sorrow at her departure is in how old we feel, thinking we have seen this kid from formula to formals, and now she is essentially an adult ... so what does that make us? *Old,* that's what it makes us! I kind of want to slap her around for that—I'm not *ready* to feel old!

I asked my grandmother once what it feels like to get older. She told me that her brain still thought the same things and felt the same feelings it did when she was twenty, but her body just refused to keep up with her brain. I am beginning to relate to that more and more.

Grandma also told me that life is not unlike a 78 rpm record. For those of you who remember vinyl records, you know that the needle seems to move relatively slowly at the beginning of the song but ever so much faster by the end of the song. And life, she said, was just like that.

When you're little you can't wait to be older, and it would seem to take forever to do so. Then, before you get turned around, your kids are grown, retirement looms, and the weeks fly by in a blur.

When it is all said and done and I reflect on my life thus far, I find that I still seek the same things I did twenty years ago: to love, be loved, feel special, and have some peace in my soul. Some of those things I have accomplished, and some are still waiting to happen. Perhaps what we need to remember is to make everyone we meet feel special each time we see them. Then truly every day we would have Mother's Day ... and Father's Day ... and Children's Day ... and Boss's Day, and ...

"We were made for each other. I needed new
luggage and he came with a lot of baggage."

Chapter 19
Men—"You Can't Live with 'Em And You Can't Shoot 'Em"

I heard someone say that once, and I thought it was so hilarious that it has become my credo regarding some of those of the male gender. I find it also applies nicely to children, pets, bosses, and anyone else who happens to irritate me at any given moment.

My neighbor next door, Deb, has an adolescent daughter who has recently become interested in the opposite sex. We know that because she was seen necking with some local Don Juan at Indiana Beach, an amusement park once known around here as the "Riviera of the Midwest." The two of us began hitting her with all of the reasons she should never get involved with a man.

1. Men will expel air from the darndest places at the most inopportune times and locations.
2. Men will attempt to run your life, sometimes without knowing they are really doing it.
3. Men will leave their socks and dirty underwear everywhere.

4. Men only want one thing (good grief, we really *have* becomes our mothers!) .

5. Not only will men love you and leave you, but they will most probably impregnate you with a child that will become just *like* them!

The list went on but you get the gist. She simply smiled and walked away, probably thinking we were both out of the loop and had become just a couple of cynical middle-aged ladies. Feeling our job in guarding her virtue was probably in vain, we popped open a couple of wine coolers and began to compare notes as to where exactly we would have been had we listened to this tired old lecture when it was first delivered to us.

Yes, back then we believed that love was the most important thing in marriage. Now we know it takes a whole lot more. If I am ever again in the market for a potential friend/lover/spouse, I will require the following things:

1. A clean bill of health from the physician of my choice
2. A financial statement
3. An application form with a seventeen-point quiz

Most of my friends think this is carrying things a bit far, but I happen to think it is just good business sense. The first time I may have suffered from Clue Deficit Disorder, not knowing exactly what I needed besides the love of my life, but now I have a slightly expanded view of what I want and need. I think the application form could be interesting and rather fun. It might go something like this.

APPLICATION FOR ENJOYMENT

1. Position desired: (Circle one) Friend / Lover / Spouse / Other
2. Number of previous marriages: _____
3. Number of current dependents (to your knowledge): _____

The following are multiple-choice questions. Please answer them as you really feel and not how you think I want you to answer. Remember, some of the answers can be crosschecked by examining your financial statement.

4. I like my women to: (Circle all that apply)

   (A) Be seen and not heard
   (B) Be like my mother with a better body
   (C) Involve me in every facet of their lives
   (D) Be able to think and act for themselves without bothering me all the time

5. My laundry goes:

   (A) Where I take it off
   (B) Wherever my friend/lover/spouse says it should go
   (C) Directly into the laundry room and/or washing machine
   (D) In the trash

6. It's Super Bowl Sunday and I want to go to the movies. You want to watch the game. You would: (Be *honest* now!)

   (A) Go to the movies, but grumble under your breath the whole time
   (B) Tell me you've seen the movie and it stinks
   (C) Fake an illness and tell me to go without you

(D) Record the game on your television and watch it later

(E) Tell me how important this game is to you and ask if you could please take a rain check on the movie

7. How many times would you use the ploy asked in question 6?

(A) Every time there is a game I want to see

(B) Only if the Chicago Cubs were in the World Series

(C) Never–I hate sports

8. We've just had a terrible fight and aren't speaking. What will you do next? (Circle all that apply)

(A) "I'm going to Disney World!"

(B) Shower me with candy, flowers, and diamonds

(C) Call me and apologize, even if it was my fault

(D) Assume that when I want to end the fight I'll let you know

9. I have two children, ages _____ and _____. How do you feel about this?

(A) I am not intimidated at all and look forward to the challenge.

(B) Oh well, what's two more?

(C) I am somewhat intimidated, wondering whether they will like me or will burn me at the stake.

(D) This is somewhat of a problem: How often do they go to their father's or friends' houses?

(E) This is a serious problem. I don't like kids—mine or anyone else's!

10. Which of the following interests are you willing to share with me? (Circle all that apply)

(A) Antiques   (G) Cooking—you cook, I watch

(B) Books   (H) Domestic engineering (i.e., chores)

(C) Jewelry   (I) Computers

(D) Traveling   (J) Karate

(E) Creative writing/art   (K) Bowling

(F) Refinishing furniture   (L) Flea Marketing

11. What interests would you like me to share with you?

   _____

12. How often do you think a couple should have sex?

   (A) What are you doing right now?
   (B) Every day
   (C) Whenever I have enough energy
   (D) On your birthday, Christmas, etc.
   (E) Whenever there is a lunar eclipse

13. I snore only:

   (A) On nights when you don't
   (B) On nights when you do
   (C) On days ending with the letter "y"
   (D) Never

14. My idea of a pet is: (Circle all that apply)

   (A) Someone else's
   (B) One dog and/or one cat, never more than that at one time
   (C) A goldfish that I will take total responsibility for
   (D) As many animals as my house (and income) can take care of
   (E) I hate pets

15. My dog (supposing I do indeed have one) has just ripped up the couch, the recliner, most of the kids' toys, and the cord

off the new window blind, bathed in the creek, and is now sitting in your lap. You would: (Circle the most appropriate answer for you)

(A) Sweetly request the dog vacate your lap
(B) Send the dog into the next lunar orbit
(C) Say, "That's okay" and let him have the recliner
(D) Build the dog his own fenced-in spot in the yard, complete with his own dog house, with window air-conditioner

16. How do you feel about filling out this application form? (Circle all that apply)

(A) Humiliated and degraded
(B) Think this woman must be a very entertaining and creative woman
(C) Think some of this stuff is none of your business
(D) Ashamed I didn't think of this myself
(E) Wish I had thought of this myself—sure would have saved me a lot of unnecessary dinners!

17. References: (May not include your mother, who will always swear you were "a perfect child," or your father, who will always say you were "shiftless and lazy," or your siblings, who will always swear that "Mom liked you best")

Name   Phone #   What You Think I Am Most Likely to Be Told

_____

_____

_____

Okay, I realize that finding a man willing to provide me with what I want is a million-to-one shot, but you have to admit that if

I were able to find someone like this, he would be worthy of deep respect and would be a treasured find indeed. Perhaps I'll give this questionnaire to my husband and see how close he would come if he really knew what I wanted.

Men … perhaps you really *can* live with them … then you wouldn't *need* to shoot them!

Chapter 20

The Greatest Kid
Stories Ever Told

Art Linkletter was a famous comedian in the 1960s era. He hosted a television program called *Kids Say the Darndest Things*. On this show he proved the adage that "kids will tell the truth … usually at the most inopportune moments."

While a kid may wander away from you in a store at the slightest provocation, you can bet he'll be standing right next to you when he mutters, "Boy, is that the ugliest guy you've ever seen or *what?*" usually loudly enough for everyone nearby (and usually the one being referred to) to hear in detail. That's the time when I fervently wish for a Popiel Pocket Black Hole Kit, so that I might step into it and never be seen again.

However, kids are inherently amusing little creatures. Almost every parent worth his or her salt has a great kid story to tell, and of course, we all think that our story is the best. One night, when my youngest son was seven, he told me a make-believe story about "Plucky the Platypus," about a little dinosaur. It had been a long day, and as I lay down on the bed beside him, I felt myself nodding off as the story became longer and longer.

Suddenly I heard him say, "And Plucky the Platypus likes to eat dead mommies."

I looked up, startled. "Dead mommies?" I asked.

"Yeah," he said "You know, the dead mommies they wrap in toilet paper."

"You mean mummies?" I asked.

"Yeah," he replied. "Whatever." And the story proceeded …

The best kid story I ever heard, though, came from one of the girls I work with. One foggy Christmas Eve, she and her husband were returning home with their children after a Christmas party. In the distance a red beacon was flashing on and off through the fog. The eldest son looked out, saw the light, and yelled excitedly, "Dad! Step on it! *There's Rudolph!* We gotta get home *quick!*" They rushed home, and Sue said she had never seen anyone move so fast in all her life to get ready for bed. She said he moved at light speed and was asleep in five minutes flat!

Another friend and I have compared kid stories for years. She told me that one day one of her sons came downstairs after acquiring a small cut on his forehead. He asked for a Band-Aid to cover it, but since she was trying to serve coffee for her husband and a few other farm friends, she asked him to wait patiently and she would get it for him. Apparently, he thought he had waited long enough, and the next thing she knew, he came out of the bathroom wearing a self-adhesive feminine protection pad! The guys really got a charge out of that one!

I admire the patience of this woman. I could write a book about the antics of her children. Every time I get irritated with my own children, I remember that I could have had *her* kids! Not that they aren't great kids—they just have more interesting stories to relate than mine did. One day her third son came downstairs inquiring as to how one went about removing permanent marker stains from skin. She asked him what he had colored. He promptly proceeded to drop his pants and show her that he had colored his penis blue and his testicles black! After assuring that there would be no permanent damage, she told him it would just have to wear off. We hoped it would come off before he had to shower with the guys in phys ed in high school.

As a youngster my younger son was perpetually hungry. You could almost always find him with his head stuck in the refrigerator. In fact, for the longest time he thought his name was Shuthedoor, because I was always yelling into the kitchen "Hey, shut the door! You're letting all the cold air out!" At least he always got food, though; my girlfriend's kid accidentally drank the urine specimen she was using to confirm her fourth pregnancy!

Maintaining physical intimacy with children in the house is another little trick that aspiring parents should beware of. Sexual encounters need to be scheduled, planned, and sometimes procured at risk to life and limb. More specifically, they usually occur when the kids are farmed out for an overnighter or are off to Grandma's house. Sometimes when they think their children are firmly ensconced in front of the television, parents will steal off to "grab a quickie." My friends tried this once, but apparently the TV went on the fritz. Sometime after the pregame formalities, but just before the big finish, my friends looked up to see their daughter standing beside the bed staring at them. Her only comment was, "Fix da TB now!" So much for grand passion.

When my children were babies, I dreamed of the day when I would send them both off to school, when I could magically reclaim my life and do all of the things I had put on hold for so very long. So far I have yet to have a single day all to myself. My girlfriend told me she had the same hopes for college; however, her son called home after the third day, saying that not only had he changed his major, but he thought he would really rather be at home. She said she had heard this had happened to someone else she knew, and that after she dropped her son off at college, he actually beat her back to the house!

I asked my kids once where they thought they would like to live when they grew up. At five years of age, Jake, who has rarely been out of Burnettsville (population 450, and 25 of those are cows) announced, "I'm moving to New York City!" Nick simply stated he planned to build a house in the backyard, so that he could continue to use the pool. I asked him to try to remember in five years, when he thinks we are morons and can't wait to get away from us, that he'd said that.

I'm beginning to think my mother-in-law's definition of rearing children is essentially correct. She said, "Children are someone you worry about—no matter how tall they grow." Even she was not immune to their misinformed humor. My youngest son prided himself at an early age on being able to use larger vocabulary words to describe simple things. Admittedly, my mother-in-law was a little hard of hearing but hated the prospect of acquiring a hearing aide. After several attempts to make her understand what he was trying to say, my son finally asked, "Hey, Grandma, do you need a hearing grenade or what?" Sometimes after a particularly stressful day at work, I find myself fervently wishing for a hearing grenade, so I wouldn't have to listen to anyone else needing something I don't have to give. That might catch on ... could be the perfect Christmas gift for those people at the end of the list we never can find the perfect gift for ...

Chapter 21
From Diamonds to Divorce

I wasn't expecting to get married when I did; in fact, I'd finally gotten accustomed to the notion that a woman could have a fulfilling life without a man. And that is just when my white knight pulled up on his silver steed. Okay, it was a green BMW, and I cornered him into asking me out, but the thought process was there.

We weathered eighteen or so years together, while growing further and further apart. Then came my Big Four-Oh. Turning forty was an entity all of its own. I didn't expect to be leveled by a number, but it happened anyway. Whether it's the psychological implications of impending old age or a hormonal flux, the "midlife crisis" is a largely underrated event. I never thought that I would be the kind of person who would devote that much energy to avoiding what everyone else already knows ... that at some point you get old.

One day I took the time to really look at myself in the mirror. I saw gray hairs; I colored them. I saw wrinkles; I bought stock in Mary Kay. My neighbor told me my clothes looked frumpy; we went shopping. I couldn't get my new Victoria's Secret undies on until I lost twenty pounds; I dieted and exercised. I felt intellectually challenged; I returned to college. I hated my life; I tried a new one.

I looked in the mirror again. What I saw was a forty-year-old woman with obviously dyed hair who looked like she had raided her daughter's closet. From the looks of her face, she should have gotten the spackling compound instead of the pore minimizer. I saw a woman with dark circles under her eyes, emphasizing the late nights of studying. The "new her" was even worse than the old her.

The marriage was next. All the quirks about my husband that I had at first found clever and amusing, bound to never bore me, had become highly irritating at best, and thoroughly reprehensible at worst. He found behaviors in me that were equally disgusting to him. Our conversations became either formally polite or full of nit-picking over trivial matters. Under the "for better, for worse" clause in our marital contract, we had zeroed in on worst-case scenario.

We tried counseling; he got better, I got worse. I spent many hours examining the layered emotions of buried rage and hurts that were stuffed inside instead of ventilated. I had blamed myself for the failings of others at times, yet avidly refused to see my own culpability at others. In short, I was a mess.

He began to do laundry, cook dinner, and take responsibility for the kids. Instead of sitting in the recliner without talking to anyone, he began to take a more active interest in the family. He came out of his shell and developed new interests and talents. Instead of making me happy, it just made me madder and sadder. Once again we were walking parallel paths, but now there was a chasm between us, and the only bridge was the children.

Children are the big losers in the battle between warring parents. While we tried to keep the open disagreements from them, the tension between us was palpable. No one wanted to be at our home; we all found places to hide out. It doesn't take a rocket scientist to figure out where this scenario was headed.

By somewhat mutual consent, we elected to divorce. Divorce is more than dividing up the Tupperware and splitting the assets. It's more like the excision of your heart without anesthesia. As you struggle to disengage the roots of emotions and memories from years of living together, you may often stop to ask yourself why you're doing this and if things will ever get better or feel normal again. Mutual friends begin to avoid you as they struggle to maintain a relationship with both parties. Rumors fly as people try to find a "reason" for a divorce, trying to ascertain who is the "victim" and who is the "dirty dog." The truth is that everyone involved is a victim in the game of divorce, and nobody wins.

Once we were no longer trying to hold the marriage together, it became a lot easier to point out how we had failed each other, in graphic detail and for hours at a time. Perhaps if we could have had these conversations earlier, they might have mattered. Now all they did was worsen the depression and sense of failure. I would often retreat to a quiet corner or to bed to mourn the loss of the thing I had wanted more than life itself—marriage to the man I loved. I felt and feel this failure keenly, and I wonder if I'll ever trust myself to love another. Moreover, I am trying to redefine this thing called "love."

I find it inconceivable that people would volunteer to go through divorce more than once. This has been an emotional autopsy for me, and I cannot imagine how Liz Taylor did it so many times. Does it get easier with practice? Can you really love after that many failed relationships?

Is love really an emotion, or is it really just duty, honor, and obligation? I find it ludicrous now that I stood up in front of three hundred people and promised to love one man forever. How can you possibly know what things will happen in your life?

The statistics on divorce are dismal. It is said now that one of every three marriages will end in divorce; the figures on subsequent marriages are equally sorry. Yet we continue to try to find that "Mr. or Miss Right" that will make us happy and content.

The secret, I believe, is in learning to find the happiness that lies within yourself, and then sharing it with others. The writer Agnes Repplier said, "It is not easy to find happiness in ourselves, and it is not possible to find it elsewhere."

There will be no words of advice from this chapter. I am straining to hear the words in the winds of change. Whatever lies ahead, I merely pray for the strength to endure and for some form of peace to heal the wounds that I have received and will inflict on others.

Chapter 22
Time Marches On

It seems it is always time for something to happen. Each morning at 5:15 the alarm goes off—time to exercise. Soon it is six o'clock—time to rouse the children. A quick shower and a quicker getting dressed, and it is time for breakfast. All too soon it is 7:40—time for the bus and time for hurried hugs, kisses, "Have a good day," and "I love you."

Then it is time for work—an eternity gone in a heartbeat. Then I hurry home in time for dinner and baths and homework. All too soon it is bedtime and time for stories, for tucking in for the night, for loving hugs, kisses, "Sleep tight," and "I love you."

And time marches on. On this morning, as on every first-day-of-school morning, we will hustle the children onto the porch to commemorate the moment with a photograph. Years later we will look back and laugh to see our children frozen in time: "Here's how we looked in the first grade, second grade, third grade," and so on. I barely remember my children as babies. If it weren't for the pictures, I wouldn't be sure some of these things really happened. And so I write of these moments, to capture them in time as well, to celebrate the lives I have loved so well.

On the opening morning of my younger son's first-grade year, he brought a shiny red apple from the kitchen.

"What's that for?" I asked.

"An apple for the teacher!" he replied proudly. I figured with that sort of sucking-up technique, perhaps I should assure his future in politics.

Ever the pragmatist and not to be outdone, my elder son sauntered forth also with a gift in hand.

"What that?" I asked.

"Two dollars for the teacher," he calmly replied.

"Oh, honey," I said in dismay. "Teachers can't take tips." I inwardly groaned, imagining the new teacher would probably think he was trying to bribe his way into her good graces or perhaps into better grades.

"Why don't you take an apple like your little brother?" I said, thinking to set matters right quickly. He shook his head at me and gave me that "parents are so dumb" look.

"Maybe she doesn't *like* apples," he reasoned. "But I've never met *anyone* who doesn't like money!" I realized that with an attitude like this I would never be sure whether to enroll him in Calculus or Crooks 101 ...

Time passes so quickly. I remember my grandmother saying that I should enjoy my childhood because time went quicker the older you got. During my childhood I thought I would never grow up. Time seemed to drag on into eternity. But after my twenty-first birthday, time went by in a blur. Suddenly I look at the calendar and see that I'm forty. I'm the oldest parent in the first-grade class. Some of my classmates have children in college, while others actually are grandparents. Today I worry about midriff bulges, wrinkles, unwanted hair growth, calories from fat, creating a safe environment for my children, paying the bills, balancing a family with a career, and struggling to make more time for the things that are the most important.

Ten years from now, I'll worry about high school graduations, college, children getting married, becoming a grandmother. I'll worry about thinning hair, wrinkles the size of the Grand Canyon, osteoporosis, retirement. I'll worry about my grandchildren and hope to have enough time to enjoy watching them grow.

I admit that Harriet Nelson was the mother image I wanted for myself. But in talking with other mothers from that same time period, I find they had a lot of the same worries. Only the times have changed—the worries remain the same.

Unmarried friends ask if I regret marriage and children. I guess it all depends on which day you ask me. But when all is said and done, I wouldn't have missed some of the experiences of this lifetime for anything in the world. One of the finest gifts we are given in this life is the ability to laugh and to love … "and the greatest of these is love."

When You Thought I Wasn't Looking

I know there were times when we weren't there for you:
Times when work beckoned, or when self-centered interests
Took us away from you.
There were days when tear-filled eyes said,
"Don't go, Mommy!" You probably thought I didn't see them. ...
But when you thought I wasn't looking,
I cried all the way to work.

There were times when you rushed into the house
Ready to tell me all about your day.
Some days I'd be busy with another project
(or on the phone!), and I would tell you, "Just a minute!"
You would walk away and busy yourself with something else.
But when you thought I wasn't looking,
I saw the disappointment in your eyes.

There were times when you thought we were too rough on you,
When your friends were allowed to do what you were not.
You thought our expectations of you were too great.
We knew only too well the perils and pitfalls of this life,
But even a mother bird must eventually
let her young leave the nest.
So we would close our eyes and let you try, unsure of
Whether you would fall or fly.
And when you thought I wasn't looking,
My heart soared each time you flew.

There were times when you cried because you thought
You had failed us or yourself.

There were times when friends and family let you down,
And your anger knew no bounds; you thought no one cared.
Your words spoke volumes of the pain and loneliness within,
And when you thought I wasn't looking,
My heart caught every tear.

So I saved each scrap and token of the life that you have lived.
To mirror the past with memories so you
can see just where you have been.
And I hope one day you'll see yourself as I have seen you …
A young man with the greatest potential for success.
Remember that life is not so much about the trappings of this life
But of the love you have within and share with others.
I hope you will someday know the tremendous love
Of a parent for a child,
And the sappy joy you feel for a dandelion presented just to you,
Or a homemade card made with paper and glue.
So when you look through this book, I hope you will see
That when you thought I wasn't looking,

THIS is what I saw …

Love,
Mom
~ Given at high school graduation to my sons

Chapter 23
Delving through the Dust

I have tried to publish this book several times through the years. It was rejected repeatedly. So I would put it away and then periodically write a chapter here and there.

Recently, I was asked to write a column for a local paper, and I found I still love to write and share my thoughts with others. Since I was on a roll, I thought I'd try to publish this work again. Imagine my surprise when I discovered that I had written this book on a Mac and the floppy wouldn't convert to PC.

So I have spent the past several nights rewriting it. I had thought to try to bring it into the present tense and then thought better of it. At this point you have shared motherhood with me over the course of more than twenty years. Not much has changed in terms of my thinking … only what has happened with the time in between.

Since the last chapter I have remarried to a man I will call my best friend. To my absolute surprise he actually provided evidence of his health, was absolutely honest about his finances, and even agreed to take the quiz! (Obviously, he passed.) This relationship is a very different one from the first. Maybe it's because he has also suffered through a painful divorce. Maybe he didn't ask enough questions in the first place either.

After many years of struggles, I can tell you that upon occasion my ex-husband, my current husband, and I can actually sit on the deck, have a drink together, and spend time with the kids in the same room, and we can do so without rancor. That has taken some tremendous growth on all of our parts, but it really is the best course of action for all concerned.

The elder son, who vowed to build a house on our property, now lives in San Diego, halfway across the continent.

The younger son, who swore he would move to New York City, then later to New Zealand, is still in Indiana for the time being, but I imagine that will change once his master's program is completed.

The house is quiet, pictures on the wall the only way you would know that a bustling family once lived here. All that time I wished to have for myself is now spent wondering when I'll get to see my kids again. Funny, isn't it?

As for me, I continue to write about life and love, just in a different manner. The column I'm working on has made me think of all the words I've written before, now lying in the dust of bookshelves, drawers, and boxes. It has been wonderful in retyping this manuscript to relive some of the family events I thought had been relegated to ancient history.

All in all, it's been a good life. Glad I could share it with you. Thanks for reading it.

May your own motherhood story be just as glorious. Do yourself a favor and write your memories down. It's amazing how many of them we forget.

There have been many joys and many disasters in this thing called life, but of them all I believe motherhood was my favorite natural disaster. May it be yours as well!

A Mother's Heart Song

I am the Lord's babysitter;
I work for the Heavenly Juvenile Court.
He has entrusted two children to me.
But I can only watch these children
Laugh and play and run—they are not mine.
I can only teach those things
That will help them on their way.
Someday He'll come back
To reclaim His children.
And I will be left with an empty spot
Where these two have been.
When I look again, they will have changed.
For they will be His babysitters,
And I will be retired.

~1989

Acknowledgments

Randy Glasbergen cartoons—reprinted with permission

Family Circus cartoons by Bil Keane—reprinted with permission through King Features Syndicate.

CPSIA information can be obtained at www.ICGtesting.com
Printed in the USA
LVOW130903270313

326202LV00001B/6/P